Nick Bunker is the author of *An Empire on the Edge: How Britain Came to Fight America*, *Young Benjamin Franklin: the Birth of Ingenuity* and *Making Haste from Babylon: the Mayflower Pilgrims and their World*. In 2015 *An Empire on the Edge* won the George Washington Prize in the United States and it was a finalist for the Pulitzer Prize for History. In 2010 *Making Haste from Babylon* was longlisted for the Samuel Johnson Prize for Non-Fiction. A graduate of King's College, Cambridge, and Columbia University, Bunker lives in Lincolnshire with his wife Susan and their otterhound, Champion Teckelgarth Mercury.

ALSO BY NICK BUNKER

Making Haste from Babylon: The Mayflower
Pilgrims and Their World

An Empire on the Edge: How Britain Came to
Fight America

Young Benjamin Franklin: The Birth of Ingenuity

NICK BUNKER

The Mayflower Pilgrims

VINTAGE

2 4 6 8 10 9 7 5 3 1

Vintage
20 Vauxhall Bridge Road,
London SW1V 2SA

Vintage Classics is part of the Penguin Random House
group of companies whose addresses can be found at
global.penguinrandomhouse.com

Penguin
Random House
UK

Selection copyright © Nick Bunker 2020
Selected from *Making Haste from Babylon*
© Nick Bunker 2010

This short edition was first published in Great Britain
by Vintage Classics in 2020
Making Haste from Babylon was first published in
Great Britain by The Bodley Head in 2010

www.vintage-books.co.uk

A CIP catalogue record for this book is available from
the British Library

ISBN 9781784876494

Typeset in 11.5/13.75 pt Bembo
by Integra Software Services Pvt. Ltd, Pondicherry

Printed and bound in Great Britain by Clays Ltd, Elcograf S.p.A.

Penguin Random House is committed to a sustainable future
for our business, our readers and our planet. This book is made
from Forest Stewardship Council® certified paper.

MIX
Paper from
responsible sources
FSC® C018179

CONTENTS

Contents

AUTHOR'S NOTE

A pest, a fanatic and a hypocrite, worse than a cattle thief: that was a Puritan, said King James I of England. Despite his many talents, the king had many flaws, and we cannot trust him to describe men and women whom he loathed. We have to find a less insulting way to define them, briefly but with fairness. Without such a definition, what follows will make very little sense.

The word 'Puritan' first appeared early in the reign of Queen Elizabeth, in about 1565. Puritans were people who believed that she failed to go far enough when she established a Protestant Church of England. They urged her to abolish every last trace of Roman Catholic ritual that still lingered within it. They also wished to see an end to the hierarchy of bishops that the queen had left intact.

Her Majesty had not the slightest intention of agreeing to these demands. So, if Puritans could not have the kind of official religion they wanted, they chose to look for God in private. As the law required, they went to their parish church every Sunday, but at home they prayed, discussed sermons, and studied the Bible.

Mainly, Puritans read the book of Genesis, the letters of Saint Paul, and the Psalms. In the New Testament, they also paid special attention to the Acts of the Apostles. Here they found the story of the early Church, and a portrait of Christianity in what seemed to be its most authentic form. Free from distortion by popes and cardinals, it offered a model they felt obliged to copy.

Before the English Civil War, almost every single Puritan was also a Calvinist. What did this label signify? It meant that they followed the teachings of the French reformer John Calvin, who died in 1564.

For Calvin, God was an absolute monarch, a king who created the universe and then sustained it at every moment by a supreme act of will. But if God was almighty, and foresaw everything that occurred, then before the beginning of time he must have decided already the fate of each human soul. This was called the doctrine of double predestination.

Like Calvin, English Puritans believed that God had divided the human race in two. Before they were born, those chosen to receive the gift of faith were set apart for eternal life. They were called the elect. The remainder of humanity were doomed to punishment forever. Try as they might, they could never obtain salvation, and so they were known as the lost.

Did these ideas make men and women fatalistic? If human beings could not change the mind of God, why bother with faith, hope and charity at all? In fact, Calvinists reached the opposite conclusion. If Christians wanted to be sure that they belonged to the elect, it was all the more important to do good deeds and to worship correctly. To persevere in holiness gave them the best evidence that they were saved.

Among the Puritans in England, some of those who persevered the most were a small minority known either as Separatists or as Brownists, after the founder of their movement, Robert Browne. In terms of theology, Separatists were strict Calvinists too, but they carried Puritan beliefs as far as they would go. They argued that the Church of England was beyond redemption because of its Roman Catholic past. In their eyes, it bore the marks of Satan, not those of Jesus Christ.

Because of this, Separatists felt compelled to do more than read and pray in private. They decided to leave the established Church entirely and set up alternative congregations. Untainted by the influence of Rome, these assemblies would be pure in their membership, and in the way they worshipped. In 1593, Parliament and Queen Elizabeth made Separatism a crime. Three decades later, a band of refugee Separatists would sail to America on the *Mayflower* to create the Plymouth Colony on the coast of what is now the state of Massachusetts. The *Mayflower* passengers of 1620 were the people whom history has come to know as the Pilgrims.

1

ELIZABETHAN ROOTS

The Wrath of God

Nothing would bee done for a Plantation until some hundred of your Brownists of England, Amsterdam and Leyden went to New Plimouth.

—Captain John Smith,
*True Travels, Adventures,
and Observations* (1630)

Easter week in 1580 was far hotter than usual. On Wednesday, 6 April, at six o'clock the working day was finished, and the English were eating, drinking, or at play: or, if they were devout, they might be listening to a midweek sermon, as they were in a church opposite Newgate Prison. Later, it was claimed that boatmen felt a strange unquietness in the waters of the Thames. If so, it was the only sign that anything was wrong.

Suddenly, on the south coast, people heard a detonation like the firing of cannon at sea. For weeks, the locals had been readying defenses against the danger of a Spanish invasion. Perhaps, for an instant, they feared that this was the first salvo of a bombardment. Before the noise died away, the ground began to move under the impact of the most severe earthquake to strike England for more than a century.

It began when a fault slipped twenty miles beneath the Strait of Dover, sending shock waves south to Normandy and as far north as York. As it ended, Londoners heard ragged chimes from a hundred parish churches, as the tremor caused the bells to ring a disorderly peal. Some panicked, like lawyers dining in the Inns of Court, who ran out into the street with their knives still in their hands. Others blamed their quivering wainscots on rats or weasels. The earthquake lasted less time than it took to say the Lord's Prayer.

Only two people died. One was a shoemaker's boy, killed by a falling stone as he sat beneath the minister at Christ Church, Newgate. A serving girl beside him succumbed to her injuries later. Apart from that, damage was modest: a church tower in Kent cracked from top to bottom, flooding on the French coast, and a fallen wall at Dover Castle. But although it ranked low on the

Richter scale, in the Elizabethan mind the tremor became another dreadful warning of punishment for sin.

Separatism took shape during this period, the early 1580s, when its protagonist, Robert Browne, achieved notoriety. Some of those who travelled on the *Mayflower* were at school, at university, or starting apprenticeships: at least seven of her passengers were already aged between eight and eighteen. Exposed to new ideas taught by young schoolmasters, by equally youthful academics, or by preachers from the pulpit, they were also far more likely to be literate than earlier generations.

Two-thirds of yeomen and tradesmen in eastern England could read, twice as many as two decades previously, and this was the social group and region from which most of the *Mayflower* Pilgrims came. The content of what they read made its mark as they responded to something that felt like a crisis. In the reactions to events such as the earthquake, we find a *Mayflower* mentality developing, a state of mind in which some men and women might feel compelled to seek radical alternatives to the status quo.

Within twenty-four hours, a printer of sheet music rushed out a godly ballad, 'moving us to repent by ye example of ye earthquake'. Fifteen earthquake pamphlets appeared, with the same dire message at their heart, and the queen's bishops composed an earthquake prayer for obligatory recital. Was the England of 1580 an especially wicked place? The shaken kingdom had many reasons to feel precarious.

England was Protestant, but its religious independence dated back only fifty years, since Henry VIII broke from Rome. When Elizabeth became queen, after the death of her Catholic sister, Mary, she restored the Protestant faith, but even so the Reformation remained incomplete and unsafe. Menaced from within by covert Roman Catholics, by vagabonds, and by the idle poor, England was threatened from outside by Philip of Spain, by the Jesuits, and by their truculent henchmen, the Irish. Or so it seemed to Queen Elizabeth and her Privy Council.

In February, they ordered ships back to their ports, to be ready against a Spanish assault. A few weeks before the earthquake, they told every county in England to draw up muster rolls of available armed men. When a Catholic earl began an insurrection in Ireland, word reached London that Spanish warships were gathering, heading perhaps for Bantry Bay, to join the rebels in kicking down England's back door.

Fears about the succession added another twist of alarm. Mary, Queen of Scots lived in restless captivity in the north of England, waiting if Elizabeth died to assert her own solid claim to the Crown. Unmarried, Elizabeth had no uncontested heir of the Protestant persuasion. Worse still, she was considering a marriage with a Catholic, the Duke of Anjou, brother of the king of France. Until it was abandoned in 1582, this project came and went for four years of fitful negotiation, causing all sorts of trouble. As we shall see, it helped engender new ideas about politics, ideas that flowed into Separatism and came to influence the Pilgrims.

Why did the Anjou proposal anger the Protestant gentry? Because it put at grave risk the informal constitution by which they, and England, had come to be governed. This rested on a few simple assumptions. Gentlemen would be loyal to the queen, defend the realm, pay modest taxes and enforce the law, serving as justices of the peace, the local representatives of the Crown. In return, the JPs would run their localities as they saw fit, free from interference by cardinals, monks and foreigners. They would also keep, of course, the Church property that they had acquired since King Henry dissolved England's monasteries.

At the apex of the system sat the queen, supreme but not omnipotent, obliged to listen to advice, ignore it though she often did. To make laws, and raise taxes, she had Parliament to help her, but more relevant were her privy councillors, and they were led by two evangelical Protestants, Lord Burghley and Sir Francis Walsingham. Burghley was the queen's lord treasurer, and Walsingham served as secretary of state.

A royal marriage with a papist threatened to break the unwritten rules of the kingdom. A French consort might bring with him toleration of Catholics, and new competitors for royal favour and the rewards of public office. That, perhaps, was why, in the months before the earthquake, the Privy Council read seething letters from Protestant squires, such as one who warned of the 'serpentine subtlety' of the French and the 'inevitable danger ... of bondage, agreed upon by that holy father, the Pope'. In private, Walsingham said much the same, while Burghley bided his time.

Walsingham remembered that Anjou's mother had ordered the murder of the French Protestants, known as the Huguenots, on the feast day of Saint Bartholomew eight years before. Might such an atrocity occur in England too? What if Elizabeth died in childbirth, and Anjou seized power as a regent, raising the child in the Roman faith? Fears of a second massacre of Saint Bartholomew lingered all the more strongly, since refugee Huguenots had fled from France and settled in

England. They made friends with Walsingham and his Puritan allies, they told stories about persecution, and they wrote books expounding their ideas.

Such were the obsessions of the time. 'God hath spoken unto us these many yeares, so many wayes, by the troubles of his Church, by the Slaughter of his Saints,' wrote one author. 'By monstrous births, by strange shapes ... by foreign warres abroad, by tumults at home, and now of late by an Earthquake ... there remaineth nothing now but the day of our Visitation. The Lord will come in his wrath, to iudge and punish us.' For some, however, the earthquake might also be a call for action, a commandment to complete the work of Reformation, in a land where it remained at risk. That was what being a Puritan meant.

Puritans

For five centuries or so, since the Norman Conquest or before, England had lived a double life. Unified from the centre by the Crown, and later by Parliament too, out in the provinces the kingdom divided itself into enclaves. The Church, the state, and the economy took a honeycombed, cellular form. They consisted of overlapping units, layered one over the other: the diocese, the county, the archdeaconry, the hundred, the borough, and the town with a weekly market. At the base of this system lay the most fundamental cell, the parish, with usually a single village as its nucleus.

England had nine thousand parishes, each with a church and a minister, known as a rector or a vicar. If he were lucky, the minister lived on tithes paid by his parishioners, equal to a tenth of the gross produce of the land: grain, pulses, livestock, and everything else. If he were less fortunate, the tithes belonged to a local landowner or perhaps a college at Oxford or Cambridge, and the minister received only what they chose to give him. Money matters of this sort caused frequent quarrels, and so did another feature of the system: the fact that, in many parishes, the landowner or some other lay outsider also owned the right to nominate the minister. A parish and its tithes became property to be bought, sold, rented out, or mortgaged, by people motivated by ambition or greed as much as by religion.

In theory, beneath the queen the Church was uniform and regimented, with every parish worshipping identically. The Book of Common Prayer set out in detail the order of service. Ministers had to wear caps and white linen surplices, make the sign of the cross at baptism, and marry couples with a wedding ring. Worshippers knelt to receive Holy Communion. These old Catholic habits aroused the most frequent Puritan opposition. In practice, however, the Church was far less unified than it might seem, and rules were often bent or ignored.

In some parishes in London, in the universities, in seaports, and in market towns in the eastern counties, Protestant reform had advanced the furthest. There, where the landlord studied Saint Paul and Calvin, or hired a man who did, religion meant the preaching of the Word. In such a place worship centered on the sermon, not the Eucharist. To give sermons a sharper bite, reformers borrowed from Switzerland a new practice, called 'prophesying'. It referred to a meeting where clergy, and very occasionally laypeople, assembled to discuss the sermon's meaning, to fast, to study the Bible, and to pray aloud.

This was Puritanism. The word entered the dictionary as an insult, coined by a Catholic to make fun of hot Protestants who wished to do away with every last trace of Romanism. Puritans preferred to give themselves other labels: 'professors of the Gospel', 'professors of sincerity', or simply 'the godly'. They did not necessarily have special beliefs about God: Puritans were Calvinists, but so too was everyone else, at least in theory. Double predestination formed part of the Church of England's Thirty-nine Articles of Religion.

Instead, people recognised Puritans by the way they acted, by the tone of their voices, and most of all in their demands for a new constitution for the Church. Puritans did not simply read Calvin. They wished to create a Calvinist society, with religious assemblies based on the Swiss and French Reformed churches that he inspired.

Of course not everyone wanted to be a Puritan: they were a distinct minority. Roman Catholics fought a rearguard action from sandbagged fox-holes in remote locations. Even non-Catholics could blunt the edge of Reformation by choosing to cling to old ways or by ridiculing the godly. Many parishes lacked piety of any kind. In the middle of the century, recruitment of ministers had collapsed. Henry VIII had stripped the Church of assets, inflation shrank the value of clerical incomes, and religious strife made the priesthood a dangerous calling. In the 1570s, 80 per cent of congregations never heard a sermon, for lack of competent men. By the early seventeenth century, preachers had been found for more than half the parishes in England; but the process was slow, many doubted the need for reform, the Church was divided, and Elizabeth could not force her subjects to cohere.

Her revenues were small, and so the queen ruled by bluff and propaganda. She did so by way of favours granted and gifts received, by manipulation, and by sometimes reluctant consent, but also by way of occasional acts of extreme violence. These were sometimes effective, but often caused more problems than they solved. Faction and feud helped to determine the course of events as bishops and courtiers rose and fell in her favour. Like a pendulum, the queen's authority in matters of religion often swung well clear of the ground. Sometimes the local bishop or archdeacon had Puritan leanings, or was simply idle or easily bullied by a local landowning elite. With patrons such as these, a professor of sincerity might hope to flout the rules of worship. But, like a pendulum, sometimes the queen's demands for due order came hurtling back.

Most famously, in 1576 she ordered a ban on prophesying, because it might be subversive. She suspended Edmund Grindal, the Archbishop of Canterbury, who had dared to defend it. With Grindal in disgrace, she began to promote conservative bishops who made Puritans toe the line.

One such man was Edmund Freke, the bishop of Norwich. In the spring of 1581, he heard about a young evangelist called Robert Browne, who had begun to preach illegally in the countryside around the Suffolk town of Bury St Edmunds. Freke had him arrested, and reported the affair to

Burghley. Browne was spreading 'corrupt and contentious discours', said Freke, at gatherings of 'the vulgar sorte of the people ... to the number of an hundred at a tym in privat howses & conventicles'. This was Separatism. In Robert Browne we see it take incendiary form, as a creed in which politics and faith were intertwined.

Robert Browne and Separatism

Robert Browne was a radical through and through, brilliant but volatile. Born in about 1550 into a prosperous family of landed gentry near the Lincolnshire town of Stamford, he ended his days in prison in 1635 after he punched a parish constable who came to collect a local tax. Known sometimes as 'Troublechurch Browne', he was described by one opponent as a 'pestilent schismatic' because he mixed with his social inferiors and incited disobedience. Browne represented the most radical wing of the Puritan movement. In the following century his Separatist ideas were revived and put into practice not only by the *Mayflower* passengers who sailed to America, but also by the revolutionaries of the 1640s. It is hard to say whether or not Oliver Cromwell himself was a Brownist – he was too political to allow himself to be pinned down about the finer points of his creed – but there were Brownists in abundance in Parliament's New Model Army during the English Civil War.

When and where had Browne become a radical? In his student days at Cambridge University, where Puritanism had become an intellectual fashion as well as a religious creed. While Browne was at the university, the leading Cambridge Puritan was a young professor, Thomas Cartwright, who in 1570 gave a controversial lecture series calling for an end to the hierarchy of the Church of England. Cartwright was a Presbyterian. He called for a new, streamlined, more democratic type of church, consisting of congregations modelled on the early Christian assemblies described in the New Testament, free from the authority of bishops, but managed by a partnership between the parish clergy and powerful lay elders.

Not only did Cartwright make some influential friends, including the queen's old favourite Robert Dudley, Earl of Leicester, who saw Puritans as patriots, committed to the anti-Catholic, anti-Spanish cause. He also cast his spell over many young Puritan clergymen who fanned out from Cambridge, found positions as rectors, vicars or curates, and tried to put Puritan ideas into practice in parishes where the local gentry were sympathetic. But Cartwright had deeply offended the authorities. Dismissed from his professorship and forced out of Cambridge in 1571, Cartwright went into exile. He settled in the Swiss city of Geneva where the Calvinists were in control.

Graduating from Cambridge in 1572, at first the young Robert Browne intended to become a clergyman, but like Cartwright he found it impossible to accept the hierarchy and the rituals of the established church. In Browne's eyes, they were tainted by Catholicism and Anglican bishops were as wicked as the Pope in Rome. However, while Cartwright never abandoned the hope that one day the Church of England might be reformed by the queen and Parliament to suit his ideas, Browne decided that it was entirely beyond redemption. Apart from absorbing Cambridge Puritan ideas, Browne had also been exposed to still more radical thinking. He had read the works of French Huguenots who had actively taken up arms against the Catholic monarchy in France.

Like some of the most radical Huguenots, Browne came to believe that a Christian church had to consist of entirely independent congregations. Each one would be free to choose its minister and to worship and believe as it saw fit. He wanted to create congregations such as this immediately, without waiting for reform from above. And at times, when his rhetoric was most extreme,

Browne also came close to advocating armed rebellion against any monarch – including perhaps Queen Elizabeth – who stood in the way of the Puritan movement. Much later, Huguenot ideas would resurface with devastating effects in the England of the 1640s.

Briefly Robert Browne worked as a schoolmaster, but soon he too was dismissed. He underwent what seems to have been a spiritual crisis and then, at about the time of the earthquake of 1580, he and a fellow Cambridge graduate called Robert Harrison took the drastic step that would make Browne a byword for scandalous heresy. First they broke the law by refusing to attend Sunday services at their parish church. Then in Norwich – at that time, England's second largest city – they gathered a group of supporters and formed their own little assembly. 'There was a day appointed and an order taken,' Browne wrote later. 'They gave their consent to join themselves to the Lord in one covenant and fellowship.' This was the first English congregation of Puritan Separatists.

Leaving Norwich before Bishop Freke could intervene, Browne and Harrison headed for Bury St Edmunds and its hinterland. There they began to preach in houses, barns and in the fields. It was an ideal location to choose, because this part of Suffolk was a Puritan stronghold dominated by local landowning gentlemen who had adopted Thomas Cartwright's ideas. They wanted to make Bury into an English version of Calvinist Geneva, rigidly disciplined by a Presbyterian church run by themselves and the Puritan clergy. So the landed gentry turned a blind eye to Robert Browne's activities. Soon Browne and Harrison began to recruit more followers with fiery sermons that warned of hellfire for anyone who dabbled with the Antichrist by using the ritual and prayer books of the Church of England.

In 1581, the bishop caught up with the two men, arrested Robert Browne and sent him to London to be questioned by Lord Burghley. As it happens, Burghley was a kinsman by marriage of the Browne family. He was also reluctant to antagonise the Puritan landowners whom he found politically useful. They spoke up for Robert Browne, and so Burghley let the young man off with a reprimand. Back in Suffolk, Browne and Harrison promptly went even further by writing illegal books to be printed in the Netherlands and smuggled back into England.

At last a moment came in 1582 when the two men decided to go into exile themselves. The authorities were closing in again; and so with a few dozen followers Browne and Harrison set off for the freer climate of the Dutch port of

Middelburg, recently liberated from Spanish control. As Browne put it later, in words that foreshadowed the voyage of the *Mayflower* nearly forty years later, they 'all agreed & were fully persuaded that the Lord did call them out of England'. Meanwhile, at home in Bury, the Puritans and what was left of the Brownists continued to preach and to agitate, spreading sedition against Bishop Freke and even against Queen Elizabeth herself. The 'Bury Stirs', as the disturbances were known, came to a bloody climax in the spring and summer of 1583. The queen sent the Lord Chief Justice down from London and a purge began. Five clergymen and forty laypeople were arrested, and two men – a shoemaker and a tailor – were hanged. The books of Browne and Harrison were ritually burned at the foot of the gallows.

Eventually Browne returned from the Dutch Republic after quarrelling with his followers. In time, and assisted by Lord Burghley, he became a reluctant conformist, serving as a country vicar in Northamptonshire for forty years before his last clash with the law. However, his books and his story had made their mark. While his books circulated underground, Browne also left a network of converts and followers in London, in Norwich, and along the coast of Kent and East Anglia, including places where in the 1600s many of the early settlers of New England originated. 'Brownist' remained a familiar word, a synonym for Puritan extremist, to be uttered on the stage in plays by Shakespeare and Ben Jonson.

The events at Bury St Edmunds in the early 1580s had established a pattern that came to be repeated in other locations as the years went by. In the England of the late sixteenth and early seventeenth centuries, despite official disapproval there were enclaves where Puritans flourished. Often they had the protection of local gentry like the Puritan landowners of Suffolk. Often the authorities – the monarch, and the Archbishops of Canterbury and York – left them alone, because Catholic plotters in league with Spain posed a far more dangerous threat. But sometimes Puritan dissent took a form so alarming that the government and the archbishops felt obliged to act.

From time to time, in a pocket of the kingdom a crisis would occur when politics and local strife combined to cause a sudden collision with authority. In such a situation, the local Puritan gentry would be unable to prevent another purge from above. In such a crisis, a committed group of Puritan men and women might choose the Brownist option, becoming outright Separatists and – if necessary – going into exile in the Netherlands and eventually in America. This was very rare indeed, but it happened in the case of the *Mayflower* Pilgrims as well as Robert Browne. As we shall see, the decisive events occurred between 1605 and 1608 during the early years of the reign of Queen Elizabeth's successor, James I. They took place in the valleys of two rivers in the north of England, in a neighborhood where Puritan ideas had taken root.

Puritan Networks

The 1590s were a grim decade. In Ireland Elizabeth waged a cruel and costly war, while in England there were epidemics of plague and poor harvests that brought the kingdom close to famine. Meanwhile the Puritan movement found itself close to total defeat. In the previous decade during the years leading up to the Spanish Armada the movement had been supported by powerful allies in Parliament and at court, including Burghley, the earl of Leicester, and Sir Francis Walsingham. Even Thomas Cartwright had been able to come home from Geneva and rebuild his Puritan campaign at home. But Leicester died in 1588 and Walsingham passed away in 1590. The Puritan party at court fell into decline. Worse still for the Puritans, they had two determined enemies at the highest level of the Church of England. The two men in question were the Archbishop of Canterbury, John Whitgift, and his most diligent official, Richard Bancroft. It was Bancroft who had led the purge of the Puritans and the Brownists in Suffolk.

Acting as a sort of clerical detective, in 1589 Bancroft uncovered embarrassing evidence about Cartwright and his friends, men known as 'forward preachers': Bancroft was able to show that they were building in secret a parallel church of their own, a Presbyterian club of clergymen and their adherents among the landed gentry. When the time was right, they would step out of the shadows and remake the Church of England as a Presbyterian assembly. It would be run by preachers and lay elders, with not a trace of old Catholic ritual, not a bishop in sight, and very little role for the queen. This, said Bancroft, was sedition of a revolutionary kind.

In 1590, the Church authorities jailed Cartwright and eight other forward preachers and stripped them of their posts as parish clergy. Their lawyers mounted an excellent defense, tying the prosecution in legal knots, and in due course they were released, after three unpleasant years in prison but without the trials reaching a conclusion.

Even so, the affair dealt a body blow to the Puritan movement. And when Parliament met in

1593, Archbishop Whitgift got what he wanted, a new statute aimed directly at the most radical Puritans and Brownists. For the first time, the law explicitly banned all private religious gatherings – 'unlawful assemblies, conventicles or meetings under pretence of any exercise of religion' – and imposed harsh penalties of banishment or prison. It was also possible, argued Richard Bancroft, to use the law of sedition to send Brownists to the gibbet as he had done at Bury St Edmunds. In that same year of 1593 he engineered the hanging at Tyburn of the most famous Separatist martyr, Henry Barrow.

Despite this, Thomas Cartwright and the forward preachers had left – like Robert Browne – a deep impression. Puritan books were still read, and Puritans survived in the universities and elsewhere, despite a hostile climate. They often met bafflement, irritation or anger among their neighbours, people who liked a little Catholic ritual and preferred a lenient religion that did not demand endless devotion. The strongholds of the Puritans were quite few and far between. But although they had a narrow base, they put down deep roots. In places, there existed a critical mass of Puritan ministers and supportive local gentlemen, yeoman farmers and town tradesmen who were prepared to be disobedient even at the risk of severe punishment.

One of these Puritan enclaves could be found 160 miles to the north of London, in a district where three counties met: Lincolnshire, Nottinghamshire, and the southernmost corner of Yorkshire. The principal feature of the landscape was the river Trent, meandering down towards the great sea port at Hull. Into the Trent flowed a smaller river, the Idle, surrounded by soggy wetlands grazed by cattle. Remote though it was, the area was strategically vital. Through it ran the Great North Road that linked the capital with York and then went on to Scotland. Beside the highway and close to the county line between Nottinghamshire and Yorkshire there stood the village of Scrooby, an official station of the Royal Mail with a postmaster employed by the Crown.

It was a district that Queen Elizabeth's ministers kept under close surveillance, because Scrooby stood on what amounted to a political and religious frontier. To the north, Yorkshire and the wild country beyond it had been slow to accept the Protestant Reformation. In 1569 the Roman Catholics of the north had risen in rebellion, marching from Durham down the highway in the hope of replacing Elizabeth with her rival, Mary, Queen of Scots. The Northern Rising ended in disaster for the rebels, with 700 executed as traitors, but the authorities remained fearful of more plots and insurrections. And so in the 1570s in an effort to stamp out the Catholic resistance the Archbishop of York launched a campaign to make the north entirely Protestant. While Catholic priests were hunted down and hanged, the authorities also used more subtle ways to win over the inhabitants. Grammar schools were founded to educate boys in the English Bible, and Puritan clergymen were allowed to function as parish ministers and spread the anti-Catholic message. At Hull with the blessing of Lord Burghley the Puritans ran the town. They imposed harsh punishments on the lazy, the tipsy and the lecherous, and compelled all the residents to listen to a Puritan preacher three times a week.

Even so renegade Catholics still lingered on. In 1578, a Whitehall intelligence report called the Scrooby neighbourhood 'a dangerous place', and noted down the names of Catholic residents whom it called 'traitors, rebels, fugitives, conspirators'. But at the other end of the religious spectrum there were also a group of Puritan clergymen installed in local churches. The most eloquent and visible was Richard Clifton, rector at the Nottinghamshire village of Babworth, seven miles from Scrooby. Everyone knew he was a Puritan – in 1593, Clifton was mildly reprimanded for refusing to baptise with the sign of the cross – but the authorities made no attempt to remove him. At a national level and in London the anti-Puritan purge continued, but here on the frontier with the north the issues were not quite the same. The Catholics remained the local enemy, while the likes of Clifton could be tolerated as godly patriots whose only fault was an excess of zeal.

Richard Clifton and his Puritan colleagues gradually built a wide following in the region. By the end of the 1590s there existed a network of Puritan sympathisers – local gentlemen, lawyers, yeomen farmers, but also craftsmen and shop-keepers – which extended across many miles of country between Nottingham, Hull, Doncaster and the market town of Gainsborough on the Trent. Among the local Puritan laity the most important for the *Mayflower* story was one William Brewster, who in 1587 replaced his father as the royal postmaster at Scrooby. Cambridge educated and steeped in the ancient classics and in Puritan literature, the young man was the nephew of the Puritan mayor of Hull. Such were Brewster's connections that earlier in the 1580s he had served as an aide to one of Elizabeth's highest officials, William Davison, and accompanied him on a diplomatic mission to assist the Dutch Republic in its war against Spain. In 1620 William Brewster would sail to America on the *Mayflower* and become the spiritual leader of the Pilgrim colony in Plymouth, Massachusetts.

In order for that to happen, Brewster had first to break entirely with the Church of England and become a Separatist. In the 1590s he and his Puritan friends and allies in the Scrooby region had no reason to do anything so radical, because of the toleration they enjoyed from the authorities. In the 1600s the picture changed utterly. A new anti-Puritan crackdown began, and the man responsible was Elizabeth's successor, the Scottish King James who came to the throne of England in 1603.

Whenever the *Mayflower* drama is replayed, James I always appears somewhere on the stage, as the villain or sometimes the comic accessory, and rightly so. If James had never lived, men and women would still have migrated to America, but their precise motives and the pattern of events might have taken a very different shape. For that reason, we have to delve into the king's character, to find what lay behind his antipathies, including his hatred of the Puritans. King James was a complicated man, and his story has many facets. One way to tell it is to begin at the end, with James I on his deathbed in 1625.

2

KING JAMES AND HIS FOES

The Entrails of the King

No kingdom lackes her owne diseases.

–JAMES I, *BASILIKON DORON*
(1603)

King James's skull was so hard and so strong that the surgeon had to struggle to break it open with a chisel and a saw. He found a swollen brain packed tightly inside the thin film of cells that enveloped its surface. The white matter filled the membrane, spilling out onto the table under the surgeon's hands. He prised out the dead man's heart, and the onlookers saw that it was unusually large. They found that his lungs and gallbladder were black. One kidney was sound, but the other had dwindled to such a tiny size that the surgeon had to rummage for it in the dead man's bowels. When at last he located it, he picked out two small kidney stones.

Although the departed had passed away three months short of his fifty-ninth birthday, he was already senile in body. Gravely weakened by arthritis, King James suffered from kidney disease, and possibly he had endured a series of small strokes. It seems that a larger stroke killed him, after eight days of fever. Only his liver remained entirely normal. This the royal doctors expected, since the case notes record the feel of the organ – 'naturally good, big, bloody and strong' – when tested by hand during the king's lifetime. Despite his many years of heavy drinking, the post mortem revealed no sign of fatty liver or cirrhosis. The tissue was as fresh and healthy as a young man's.

They removed the king's vital organs and his viscera, for separate burial in a casket. Then they embalmed the cadaver and placed it inside a sheath of lead. They encased the lead box in an oak coffin, filled with spices, its surface wrapped in purple velvet studded with gilded nails and hinges. On Monday, 4 April, 1625, eight days after the death of the king at his country home in Hertfordshire, the cortege set off for Whitehall Palace. Drawn by six black horses, the hearse travelled through pouring rain some sixteen miles southward, past London to the river Thames. At last, that evening, the coffin arrived in the royal apartments, where the monarch would lie in state.

Throughout his lifetime, since his mother, Mary, Queen of Scots, last saw him when he was ten months old, the body of the king was the object of the piercing gaze of strangers, for what it might reveal about the destiny of the state. Because monarchy obliged the king to display himself to his subjects, James always dined in semi-public, in front of those admitted to the royal apartments. His love of hunting on horseback meant that he was often seen in the open air too.

Privacy of a kind existed in the bedchamber, which James said should not 'be throng & common', but instead a place where the king could meditate and speak discreetly. And yet even here he would not be alone. 'Kings' actions (even in the secretest places) are as the actions of those that are set upon the stages, or on the tops of houses,' James told Parliament in 1610, and this was literally true. In the bedchamber, Stuart kings had about them a half-dozen gentlemen-in-waiting.

So, over the course of his reign, first as king of Scotland and then after 1603 as king of England too, many thousands of people saw James. Often they wrote down their observations. For this reason, and because so many portraits survive – at least fifteen oil paintings, besides medals, busts and the like – we can re-create a remarkably reliable picture of his appearance and his mannerisms. He also bequeathed to posterity an archive of evidence about his long feud with Puritans and Separatists. Because King James wrote copiously in four languages, much of it comes from his own pen.

James published two books containing attacks on the likes of Robert Browne. In the second, titled *A Meditation upon the Lord's Prayer*, and dated 1619, James gave a pithy account of their origins. He wrote with a lucidity that modern historians would do well to emulate. 'Our Puritans are the founders and fathers of the Brownists: the latter onely boldly putting into practise what the former doe teach,' he pretty accurately said, and he threw in for good measure an insult or two aimed at what he called 'these innumerable sects of new Heresies, that now swarme in Amsterdam'.

Much earlier, in his manual of kingship called the *Basilikon Doron*, James piled up an even larger heap of abuse of Brownists and Puritans alike. Rash, brainsick and heady, vain, proud and pharisaical, ungrateful, fanatical, seditious and conceited, they were 'very pestes in the Churche & commonweale', said the king. And, in case readers failed to take the point, his editor inserted an extra little caption, calling Puritans 'an evill sorte'.

Why did James hate nonconformity so much, and why did he feel compelled to venture into print? Queen Elizabeth, a mistress of delegation, never stooped to verbal combat with Separatists: for her, a couple of public hangings every ten years did the trick quite well enough. What made James behave so differently, with less physical violence, but with so much more emotion?

He acted as he did because he wished to defend the hygiene of the realm. Aptly enough for a king who spent his later years in almost constant physical pain, James tended to speak about his kingdoms in the language of the body and medicine, in terms of anatomy, well-being and morbidity. In doing so, he did more than merely repeat medieval clichés that compared the realm and its people, the body politic, to a frame of human flesh and blood.

Men and women at the time used figurative language so freely and with such verve that it was impossible to say where metaphors finished and reality began. They did not think in terms of rigid lines of demarcation between soul, mind and body, or between matters that were personal and those that were political. In the eyes of Jacobeans, God had created everything, and so everything was connected to everything else. For them, an educated man or woman was a person who tried to see things as a whole.

So it was with King James. He never used one metaphor where five would do. 'What God hath conjoined, let no Man separate,' he said in 1604, as he urged his first Parliament to unify England and Scotland by force of law. 'I am the Husband, and all the whole Isle is my lawful wife: I am the head, and it is my body: I am the shepherd, and it is my flock, I hope therefore, no man will be so unreasonable, as to think … that I, being the Head, should have a divided and monstrous body.' In the eyes of King James, a Christian king performed the role of a bridegroom, a father and a pastor; he was God's lieutenant on earth, he was the origin of justice, and he was the source of wealth and well-being.

From the heart of the kingdom, the sovereign pumped the blood of mercy through the arteries of the state. That being so, he also served as the doctor of the nation. James called the monarch 'the proper Phisician' of his kingdom, with a duty to cure it from sickness, and this he meant entirely literally. He used the phrase not in some work of learned theory but in his most famous and practical text, *A Counter-blaste to Tobacco* of 1604, his fierce attack on the practice of smoking.

A king and a philosopher, a monarch but also a human being, James experienced dominion as an alternating condition of power and fragility. 'I am a Man of Flesh and Blood, and have my Passions and Affections as other men,' he said in

1607, and this was an understatement. Often succumbing like a Shakespearean hero to waves of emotion emitted from an obscure source, James felt the troubles of his realm in his skeleton, his nerves, and his intestines. His views about health and medicine formed a seamless whole with his wider doctrine of government, and with the ideas that caused him to loathe religious nonconformists.

King James thought of Puritans as a disease, which at its worst took the form of the Brownists. North of the border he had been obliged in the 1590s to accept a Presbyterian system of government of the Church of Scotland, but he had no intention of tolerating any such thing in England and he had no time at all for Separatism. In the spring of 1603 Queen Elizabeth died leaving James as her heir and successor. He came south to claim his throne, determined to take no nonsense from what remained of the Puritan movement.

The Hampton Court Conference

As James I made his royal progress down the Great North Road, passing through Scrooby where William Brewster was the postmaster, the English Puritans made a vain attempt to persuade him to listen to their demands for reform of the Church of England. They drafted a manifesto – the 'Millenary Petition' – which listed more than thirty changes that they wished to see.

Some came from the old Puritan agenda, such as calls for an end to the sign of the cross in baptism or to bowing at the name of Jesus. Others were economic, intended to increase the incomes of the parish clergy by ending practices such as the leasing out of tithes. The petition also contained one particular demand that neither James I nor the Archbishop of Canterbury could possibly accept.

The petitioners wanted to ease the burden of 'subscription', the rules which required that clergymen swore that the Church of England's Book of Common Prayer was entirely the Word of God. If this change were made, it would remove the most powerful weapon in the armoury of discipline. Richard Bancroft had become the bishop of London, he was Archbishop Whitgift's most likely successor at Canterbury, and he had his own project of an entirely contrary kind. He wanted a much tougher set of rules to impose moral and religious discipline, and he intended to enforce it with subscription.

However, King James did not simply reject the petition out of hand. A man who relished the exchange of ideas, he convened a debate, which took place at Hampton Court Palace in January 1604. At this event, James exploded with an infamous outburst in which he issued threats against the Puritans who attended, pledging that he would 'harry them out of the land'. This was an incident so notorious in Pilgrim history that in 1921, during American celebrations of the *Mayflower*'s tercentenary, an actor dressed up as King James repeated the same words, accompanied by bagpipes, to an audience including President Warren Harding. Time and again, writers about the Pilgrims have quoted or misquoted James, uncritically and without asking what he meant.

The sentence appears in a semi-official account of the event, approved by Bancroft, and written by a clergyman called William Barlow. He and Bancroft intended to mock and belittle the Puritans, making them out to be pedants, with the conference portrayed as a total defeat for the Puritan cause. Barlow reports James's exact words as follows: 'If this bee all, quoth he, that they have to say, I shall make them conforme themselves, or I will harrie them out of the land, or else do worse.' The most revealing clause is the first – 'if this bee all' – because Barlow wished to suggest that the Puritans were trivial, and their complaints petty.

Barlow says that James became exasperated by the leading Puritan spokesman, a wordy academic who wished to make minor amendments to the Thirty-nine Articles of Religion. This, says Barlow, seemed 'very idle and frivolous' to the king and his bored privy councillors. They relieved the tedium by laughing over an old joke to the effect that 'a Puritane is a Protestant frayed out of his wits'. The king's threat to harry them out of the land was apparently something similar. It seems to have been a heavy-handed effort in sarcasm from an irritated monarch who had endured two full days of Puritan pomposity.

As it happens, the conference was not an annihilating defeat for Puritanism. Most famously, it led to James's authorised translation of the Bible. It also gave rise to a list of small reforms, such as a pledge not to excommunicate people for trivial offenses. Measures like these helped to cool the heat of controversy, and so, after the purge of Puritans ended in about 1608, England enjoyed a decade of relative calm in matters of religion.

However, in the immediate aftermath of Hampton Court these elements of compromise paled by comparison with Bancroft's energetic attack on dissenters. Whitgift died soon after the conference, leaving Bancroft to carry on the campaign against all those who disturbed peace and good order. First he pressed ahead with inspections of every aspect of cathedral and parish life, covering drunkenness and fornication, as well as signs of religious laxity. At the same time, in 1604, the king issued two proclamations against nonconformity. He insisted that everybody follow the Book of Common Prayer to the letter.

And this was where the trouble started for William Brewster, Richard Clifton and their Puritan friends in the Scrooby region. The Archbishop of York in 1604 was Matthew Hutton, an old man close to death, who had always been lenient with Puritans whom he saw as helpful allies against the northern Catholics. He wrote to King James urging him not to be too severe, but unfortunately he also also criticised the king's favourite sport of deer hunting: Hutton pointed out that it damaged poor farmers' crops. All he achieved was to antagonise the monarch.

In February 1605, James issued Archbishop Hutton with a stern rebuke, telling him to enforce the law against Catholics and Puritans alike. The authorities in the north should act, James wrote, with 'diligence and constancy against the disobedient of the one sort and of the other'. Hutton and his colleagues had no choice but to obey. In doing so they brought to an end the many years of official complacency about Brewster, Clifton and their fellow Puritans.

In March, the archbishop's Chancery Court at York called before it five Puritan clergymen from parishes in Nottinghamshire within a twelve mile radius of Scrooby. Four of the men − including Richard Clifton of Babworth − refused to sign up to the king's loyalty test. All four were dismissed from their parishes and three of them were excommunicated, with Clifton on the list. Up and down the country the same thing was happening to other Puritan clergymen. Between 1604 and 1609 about eighty Puritan vicars or rectors were dismissed for non-conformity.

In the Scrooby region, national and local politics had come together and swept away the local platoon of Puritan ministers supported by Postmaster Brewster and his comrades. No action was taken yet against laypeople, because Richard Bancroft's new book of rules had not yet come fully into force. Indeed if matters had ended with the sacking of Clifton, the Pilgrim emigration from the area might never have occurred and the *Mayflower* might never have sailed. In 1605, nobody in the Scrooby area had yet taken the radical step of leaving the Church of England entirely and setting up a Separatist congregation. For that to happen, the locality needed its own radical preacher as compelling as Robert Browne had been in Norwich and Suffolk two decades earlier. Leadership of just such a kind soon arrived in the shape of two young Cambridge Puritans, John Smyth and John Robinson.

It would be hard to exaggerate their importance. Although he never crossed the Atlantic, John Robinson served from afar as the religious mentor of the Plymouth Colony. And if any single person can claim to have launched the Baptist faith in the English-speaking world, it was John Smyth. Born in about 1575, Robinson came from a family of yeomen farmers in the prosperous Nottinghamshire village of Sturton-le-Steeple, just across the river Trent from Gainsborough. While Smyth's precise origins are unknown the evidence suggests he came from a similar farming background somewhere nearby.

Both Robinson and Smyth had won places at Cambridge University as 'sizars', the lowest grade of undergraduate, meaning that they had to pay their way by acting as servants for wealthier young men. Both men had been brilliant scholars – Robinson lectured in Greek – and both had won fellowships at their colleges, both became ordained clergymen of the Church of England and both of them found jobs as licensed preachers. And both men were dismissed for their Puritan opinions.

In 1602, the authorities in Lincoln fired Smyth from his post as the city's official preacher; in 1603 the Archbishop of Canterbury took away his preaching license; and in 1605 a similar fate befell John Robinson when he lost his preaching post in Norwich. So he and John Smyth made their way to what they thought was a safe haven in the Trent valley where the local gentry were Puritan sympathisers. At Gainsborough, Smyth preached occasional sermons and practised medicine until, in 1606, a church court convicted him of being 'contumacious'. He was also barred from working as a physician.

And so, like Browne and Harrison twenty years earlier, Smyth and Robinson took the fateful step of Separation from the established Church. A prolific, talented writer, Smyth composed a series of books which show him undergoing a long and painful period of soul-searching, as he and John Robinson revived the ideas of Browne, Barrow, and other Separatists whose books they studied. The chronology is not entirely clear, but at some time between the autumn of 1606 and the Easter weekend of 1607 they set up two Separatist congregations.

The one led by Smyth was at Gainsborough, while Robinson's met twelve miles away at William Brewster's home at Scrooby Manor. Documents survive to show us how they worshipped. Their meetings would assemble at eight in the morning and continue until five or six in the evening, in two sessions divided by a two hour break at noon. They sang psalms, but mostly they worshipped by 'prophesying', reading a Gospel text and then standing up one by one to improvise an emotional response.

These were not small groups of downtrodden people assembling in tiny and obscure locations. Servants, labourers and children were certainly involved, but typically the Separatists whose names we know were prosperous yeomen farmers, tradesmen, or even members of the lower ranks of the landed gentry. Nor were they meeting in secret. Since Scrooby Manor was a station of the Royal Mail on a highway it would have been hard to hide the gatherings there, while Gainsborough was a large, busy town with the region's principal grain market. And so news of what was going on soon reached a wide public. 'Hear you not,' wrote an anti-Puritan author in a book printed in London at the time, 'of teachers and people in the farthest parts of Lincolnshire and Nottinghamshire who are flatly separated?' By the middle of 1607 the scene was set for a crisis, a final collision with authority that would take the Separatists into exile: at first in the Dutch Republic, and then later to America.

The Breaking Point

The spring and summer of that year were anxious seasons for King James and his ministers. Since the plague and famine years of the 1590s the condition of the rural poor had continued to worsen. This led in 1607 to the most serious popular rebellion of the reign of James I. With the price of bread rising steeply and another poor harvest expected, the Midland Rising began in Northamptonshire and Leicestershire in May and had to be crushed by force of arms. A spate of hangings followed, but the authorities remained alarmed by anything that smacked of sedition.

The fear of Catholic insurrection still lingered – Guy Fawkes and the Gunpowder Plot were a recent memory – and so when a new Archbishop of York took up his post he was under strict orders to suppress every form of religious disobedience. The archbishop in question, Toby Matthew, arrived in York in August 1607 and stepped up the attack on Catholics and Puritans alike. Hundreds of Catholics were arrested, far more than the prison cells at York Castle could accommodate. So too were a handful of Separatists from the Scrooby congregation. In December, at last William Brewster became a wanted fugitive. Toby Matthew issued a warrant for his arrest, but his officers arrived at

Scrooby to find that Brewster had gone to ground. Robinson and Smyth had vanished as well.

The events that followed closely paralleled the flight many years earlier of Robert Browne to the Netherlands. It was the obvious place of refuge. Amsterdam already harboured a small community of refugee English Separatists; the Dutch allowed many different Protestant sects to worship freely; and in the dynamic trading cities of the Netherlands there was work to be found. And so in the autumn of 1607 the Scrooby and Gainsborough congregations made a first, abortive attempt to flee to Holland by sea.

They hired a ship to meet them in a secluded spot somewhere close to the town of Boston, Lincolnshire. After a long delay the ship arrived by night, but the skipper had turned traitor. Customs officers boarded the vessel, stripped and searched the Separatists, men and women alike, confiscated their belongings and placed them under lock and key. For reasons that remain unclear, they were all released without trial after varying periods in the cells; and so they had to begin all over again.

No further attempt at escape was possible that year. The winter was atrocious: 'most miserable ... frost and snow for many weeks ... such weather as no man could travel through', as Archbishop

Matthew put it in his diary. Not until the spring could the Separatists try to put to sea a second time.

The moment came in May 1608 at the little coastal haven of Stallingborough in Lincolnshire, between the ports of Immingham and Grimsby. For what occurred we have two sources. The first is a narrative account composed by the *Mayflower* passenger William Bradford and included in his detailed history of the Plymouth Colony, written while he was the colony's governor. From the vividness of Bradford's description of the events at Stallingborough, it seems likely that he was an eye-witness. He may well have been, because the young William Bradford – he was only eighteen in the spring of 1608 – was a member of the Scrooby congregation and a protégé of William Brewster. The other source is a set of sworn depositions taken down by the Grimsby magistrates on the day after the flight from Stallingborough Haven.

The escape plan had a mastermind, a lawyer and landowning gentleman from the Nottingham area named Thomas Helwys. Like John Smyth, he is still revered by Baptists as one of the founders of their form of Christianity and as a pioneer advocate of religious liberty. It seems that Helwys was also a bold, resourceful man with a taste for adventure.

He hired a coastal vessel called the *Francis*, usually employed carrying coal from Newcastle to London, and arranged for her to dock at Gainsborough on 9 May. There she took on board fifteen Separatists, ten of whom were women. Then the *Francis* sailed down the Trent and the Humber, picking up more Separatists along the way, until she had between eighty and a hundred passengers. The plan was to rendezvous at Stallingborough with another party of Separatists, including Thomas Helwys, who had walked across country. A Dutch ship was due to meet them and take them to Holland.

But the plan had a fatal flaw: Helwys had failed to reckon with the treacherous tides and mudflats of the Humber estuary. The *Francis* reached Stallingborough, ran aground and stuck fast. The Dutch ship had arrived, and was waiting for the tide to ebb and take her out to sea, when at about 4 p.m. on 12 May Helwys and his comrades saw a troop of armed militia approaching the beach. Only sixteen of the Separatists, all of them men, managed to get aboard the Dutch ship from a rowing boat. After a long and stormy voyage they got across to Amsterdam, but Thomas Helwys, the *Francis*, her passengers and all the women and children were taken into custody.

Much later in America the incident came to be celebrated in Puritan history and folklore as a graphic symbol of courage in the face of tyranny. At the time, however, it seemed that King James and his Privy Council had almost entirely destroyed the Separatist movement in England. In the next decade, only rarely did the words 'Brownist' or 'Separatist' reappear in records of prosecutions by the authorities. And so the next chapter of the Separatist story unfolded in Holland.

In the months that followed the affair at Stallingborough, Thomas Helwys and his allies among the leadership – Brewster, Robinson and Smyth – somehow found their way over to Amsterdam. And there another crisis occurred. Their old enemy Archbishop Bancroft had always predicted that when Brownists were free to do as they pleased, their communities would splinter into a multitude of quarrelsome little sects. And this is precisely what happened.

In Holland John Smyth swerved away along a new and still more radical path. He insisted that even the rite of baptism of children carried the taint of Popery and coercion, because the infant could not give free consent. Only adults could do that, and so Smyth took what seemed to be the shocking step of rebaptising himself and his followers. He split from Thomas Helwys, and the English Separatists in Amsterdam broke into fragments as Bancroft had foreseen.

In the spring of 1609, to escape from the angry atmosphere John Robinson and William Brewster led what remained of the Scrooby congregation thirty miles down the road to the Dutch industrial city of Leiden. Among them was the Pilgrim historian, Brewster's young disciple William Bradford. In Leiden ten years later politics would catch up with them again and send them on their way to Massachusetts.

3

WHY THE PILGRIMS SAILED

Leaving Leiden

> In Leiden ... all these disorders, both in church
> and state, had their beginning.

> —SIR DUDLEY CARLETON,
> JANUARY 1618

William Bradford called Leiden a 'fair, & bewtifull
citie, and of a Sweete situation', and for some of
its residents it was. It had a vast pinnacled town
hall erected only fifteen years before the Pilgrims
arrived. For its great university it possessed a lofty
auditorium, with behind it a scientific garden for
herbs. Leiden also had intelligent civic leaders. In
1611, on the northern flank of the city, they laid
out a new town with streets and canals arranged
in a grid pattern, where they built twelve hundred
new homes for weavers and their families. In fore-
sight, this far exceeded anything undertaken in

England at the time. However, Bradford wrote in terms that were too glowing. A few pages later he makes this plain himself, as he describes the Pilgrim motives for leaving the city to go to America.

No town in Europe had industry more dynamic than Leiden's. The demand for new housing arose because the city grew at alarming speed. The university was founded in 1575, soon after Leiden survived a siege by the Spaniards. At that time it had a population of ten thousand. By 1622, the number of inhabitants had soared to forty-five thousand, thanks to floods of immigrants coming to work in its textile industry. The rulers of Leiden understood perfectly well the economic forces that made their city what it was. Their favourite artist was Isaac Claesz van Swanenburg, and in the middle of the 1590s they commissioned him to portray the source of the city's wealth in a magnificent oil painting.

Hanging today in the town's museum, the picture shows the walls and windmills of Leiden at sunset, with above them St Peter's Church, situated in the quarter where Robinson and Brewster lived. In the left foreground we see an old lady clad in dowdy woollens, coloured black, brown, and maroon. Van Swanenburg paints her shrinking backward, as if she were fading into the gloom. Front and middle stands a tall young woman, wearing a white tunic emblazoned with red crossed keys, the Leiden colours and coat of arms. She offers a welcome to a slim young girl who enters from the right. The young girl wears a bright green blouse and a billowing pink skirt. As graphically as anyone could wish, the scene explains the secret of Leiden's success.

Fresh and attractive, the girl represents the so-called new draperies, light woollen fabrics, easily cut in a variety of designs. Woven in Leiden in rolls, nearly thirty yards long, white in their raw form but dyed with brilliant colours, these fabrics were known as *says*. They weighed much less than other woollens, and their popularity reached a peak in the early seventeenth century. Middle-class people, enriched by trade or rising rents, began to want new outfits with fashions that changed from year to year. They also began to wear under-garments. *Says* were ideal for both. Beginning in the late 1570s, the city of Leiden seized control of the trade, making itself the foremost producer in Europe. This happened after the siege, when a free, fortified Leiden opened its gates to refugees, driven there by war and persecution.

The decisive episode occurred after the sack of the textile town of Hondschoote, near Dunkirk, where more *says* were made than anywhere else. In the 1560s, the weavers of Hondschoote became ardent Calvinists, pillaging churches and killing priests, and when the time came they joined the revolt against Spain. In support of the rebels a French army arrived in 1582 but the troops soon fell out with the townspeople. They sacked and burned Hondschoote, destroying nine hundred workshops, and the *say* weavers fled: some to England and to Germany, but mostly to Leiden. The city welcomed them warmly, and it gave them religious freedom: not absolute religious liberty, because that never existed in the Dutch Republic, but at least the right not to join a state church. Holland did not have one. With the weavers from Hondschoote came the coloured fabrics symbolised by Van Swanenburg's maiden.

As a result, Leiden grew rich. As the years went by and demand for its cloth grew and grew, the city continued to attract new immigrants. They came not only from Hondschoote but also from Bruges, Ghent and Ypres, and then from Antwerp after it fell to the Spanish in 1585. In due course, Leiden readily allowed the Pilgrims to settle in the city.

Robinson's group numbered about one hundred, of whom about twenty-five came from the Scrooby and Gainsborough region. They reached Leiden in May 1609, after the city politely ignored a protest from the English ambassador. Leiden had an obvious, unsentimental motive for offering them asylum, because temporarily the city had lost momentum. Between 1602 and 1604 a long epidemic killed five thousand of its inhabitants. The output of *says* fell sharply, and took several years to recover. Robinson and his colleagues arrived at a time when Leiden was starting to grow again, but remained short of labour. Most of the Pilgrims found work as artisans, and some clearly worked very hard indeed.

A case in point was William Bradford. He hired himself out to a French silk weaver, until he reached the age of twenty-one. Then he sold his land in England and used the money to start up on his own. His business went badly at first, absorbing all his capital, but by 1612 he could at least afford to buy his own small house. This was success of a kind, since only two-fifths of families in Leiden were homeowners. Bradford wove fustian, a mixture of linen and wool, and he must have done so energetically. When he sold his house in 1619, it fetched 1,250 guilders: not a large sum, but equivalent to four years' wages for a labourer. In 1623, Leiden levied a property tax on householders, and if he had remained in Holland, William Bradford would have been eligible to pay it. Only a dozen fustian weavers were affluent enough to enjoy this doubtful privilege.

Weaving was only one facet of an industry built on a multitude of roles, with slots for men, women and children, whatever their aptitude, dexterity or physical strength. So we find the English in Leiden working as processors of wool as well as weavers, and there were many other opportunities, in shearing, spinning, dyeing and 'fulling', or beating and kneading cloth in tubs or pits with fuller's earth.

Workers of each kind needed helpers and suppliers, makers of soap or shears or the lads who brought beer to quench the thirst of men combing wool, an exhausting business. Van Swanenburg painted all of this as well: in the Leiden museum, immediately opposite his allegory of the old and the new draperies, visitors will find his crowded cycle of paintings of the many stages of cloth manufacture, from the import of raw wool by sea to the sale of the final product by haggling merchants. He completed the last one in 1607, two years before the Pilgrims arrived.

Van Swanenburg portrayed a thriving, confident city, but it had a dark side that he did not expose. In a trade depression, or during a war, demand would wilt, slashing the income of textile workers, who were paid by the piece. This happened during a European slump in the 1620s. The output of *says* in Leiden reached a new peak in 1617, bobbed up and down for six years, and then collapsed. Never again did it equal the heights attained in the previous decade. The fustian trade did better, taking up some of the slack, but only after its own troubles between 1620 and 1622. Meanwhile, the price of bread in Leiden soared, more than doubling in the next ten years.

Furthermore, by coming to Leiden, a refugee found himself at the bottom of the social hierarchy. In Leiden wealth and influence belonged to very few. More than half the city's property was owned by a narrow class of no more than 250 people, led by the brewers and overseas merchants. Among them were a tiny group of the super-rich, fourteen magnates who each possessed, on average, assets worth 160 times the value of Bradford's house. In England, the typical Separatist was somebody gradually rising up the social scale, but in Holland the ladder was blocked from above. No Englishman could penetrate the clique of oligarchs who ran the towns, and neither could most of the Dutch.

Inequality in the Netherlands led to bitter antagonism. This began to take a violent shape as economic conditions worsened. After the Dutch signed a truce with Spain in 1609, weavers and brewers in Spanish-held Flanders and Brabant were suddenly free to begin to fight for market share against the Dutch towns of the north.

Competition forced weavers to make cheaper cloth, so that even during the boom years profits may have fallen despite rising sales. As wages dropped, unrest grew among the workers at their looms and in the breweries. It led to a first explosion twenty miles from Leiden at Delft.

To pay for repairs of their harbour, the authorities at Delft imposed a tax on flour in 1616. At the same time they refused to place a duty on imported wine, drunk by the rich. Working women marched on the tax collector's office, with their children at their side, beneath a flag made from a long blue skirt. They attacked the town hall, ripping up records and smashing windows, while the burgomaster hid in a back room. Order was only restored when troops arrived from The Hague, and even then the ringleaders escaped over the walls of Delft by night.

And so William Bradford lived in Holland during a period that saw an angry deepening of social division. As for the beauties of Leiden, they could certainly be found, but nearby lay insanitary squalor. Disease was yet another peril facing exiles who worked in the textile trade. People died far more often in the towns than in the country, and so a path of emigration to urban Europe might well be a road to nowhere. If the Pilgrims were to survive, they needed to break away from the sixteenth-century pattern of escape undertaken by way of industrial toil in a back street. The risks they faced if they did not were all too obvious in the stinking suburb where Bradford made his home.

Life by the Back Canal

Modern Leiden has a long, wide and crowded thoroughfare called the Haarlemmerstraat. A few minutes by bicycle north from the town hall, on the way to the railway station, the street curves from west to east through the heart of a low-lying area once known as Marendorp. Long before the Pilgrims arrived, Marendorp had ceased to be a village. By 1609, it was an industrial neighbourhood, identified by the city fathers as a place to put the smelliest textile trades, those that turned canals into sewers of effluent. Fulling was one of the most horrid, and today in Marendorp you will still find a street called Vollersgracht: in English, the Fullers' Canal.

Narrow little lanes lead northward out of Haarlemmerstraat, and among them is Paradise Alley. Walk up it, and after forty paces you come to another long street, running parallel with Haarlemmerstraat, but much quieter. It used to be called Achtergracht, or Back Canal. Even now it is obvious, from the curved surface of the pavement, that a watercourse runs beneath it. This was where William Bradford lived.

The Achtergracht was what the Dutch called a *stincknest*. Even in the seventeenth century, the authorities wanted to brick it over because it was so noxious. William Bradford's privy emptied by way of a pipe leading down into the canal. Pollution was worst by far in hollows such as Marendorp, where the canals could not drain freely. The same was true near the home of William Brewster, in an alley known as Stincksteeg, much closer to the centre of Leiden, where most of the Pilgrims lived. Only sixty paces from Brewster's doorstep was a stagnant canal, another Vollersgracht, which had to be covered over in stages after 1595, because it smelled so dreadfully.

Of course there was more to Marendorp than open sewers. It made sense for Bradford to move to the district, along with seven other Pilgrim families, because on the Haarlemmerstraat was the hall where finished fustians were inspected and displayed for sale. And close by, the city authorities had built purpose-made dwellings for the working class, two minutes from Bradford's house. They occupied a site where, in the Catholic Middle Ages, monks and nuns had lived in three cloisters in Marendorp. After the Reformation, the city confiscated their property and turned the space over to become a cattle market, a leper hospital, and then a housing project.

Between 1581 and 1606 nearly six hundred new homes for weavers appeared in Marendorp. Mostly they were very small indeed. Closest to Bradford was a complex called the Mierennest, or the Anthill, where a convent had once stood. In 1596, the authorities jammed more than sixty new dwellings into the plot that the monks and the lepers had occupied. Built of brick, with a steep roof, the weavers' cottages measured twenty-two feet by eleven, with two rooms at street level, with space for a weaving loom in the front, and a bedstead and fireplace for cooking at the rear. A ladder led up to an attic bedroom. They were cheap, letting each week for the same as it cost to feed one person with the staple diet of rye bread for seven days.

New as they were, these weavers' houses captured the ambiguities of Leiden. In a sense they were the product of enlightenment, planned and built to last. At the same time, they embodied division, holding the artisans at a distance, segregated from the wealthy, who lived on the higher and healthier ground around the Breestraat, beside a free-flowing river. Worst of all, the Back Canal harboured infection. Centuries later, in 1832, the city suffered an outbreak of cholera, spread by bacteria in water contaminated with faeces. A map of the incidence of death shows that the over-crowded weavers' lanes in Marendorp were among the worst affected. Paradise Alley and the streets around it became in time the city's most infamous slums, to be shamed as such by Dutch journalists in the 1930s. Nobody would have called them that in 1617, but even so Leiden had the makings of a death trap.

Understandably, historians have always lingered over the deaths at New Plymouth in the winter after the *Mayflower* reached America. But most of the English Pilgrims at Leiden stayed put and never crossed the ocean. They numbered about three hundred. In 1624, they faced a catastrophe of their own, the worst epidemic since the siege by the Spanish. In the space of two years, the plague killed eight thousand people, nearly one in five of the inhabitants. Among those who died was John Robinson, in the late winter of 1625: he was in his early fifties. A decade later, it happened all over again, when fourteen thousand people died in the Leiden epidemic of 1635.

William Bradford gave four reasons to explain why he and his comrades left Leiden to sail to the New World. At the top of his list was what he called 'the hardnes of ye place': poor conditions, endless work, and a harsh diet. Rye bread was eaten at Austerfield too, but there at least they could cook their own bacon, and their cows gave them milk and cheese. He also mentions a gradual weakening of morale, as in Leiden the Pilgrims aged prematurely, because of the hardships of manual labour.

Third among Bradford's grounds for departure came the burdens inflicted on children. In Leiden, they had to work from an early age. In Nottinghamshire, even the smallest boys and girls hand knitted woollen stockings, but there was a world of difference between cottage life among the open fields and the toil of fetching and carrying in cramped Leiden. Worst of all, Bradford mentions the fact that the young might take to crime, or choose to ship out on Dutch vessels bound for the East Indies. In the seventeenth century, half of those who did so never returned.

Finally, William Bradford speaks about the hopes the Pilgrims had of conveying the Gospel to America. In their eyes this had become a matter not of choice but of necessity. In 1617 and 1618, as he and William Brewster and the other Separatist leaders began to draw up their plans to plant a colony in the New World, they were not the only Protestants who felt that their form of worship and belief was in grave peril on the eastern side of the Atlantic. There were ominous signs that war was approaching in Europe, a war that might spell catastrophe for the Protestant faith. Bradford and Brewster certainly hoped that in the New World they could convert the native people to Christianity. They also regarded America as perhaps the only place where Protestantism would survive the calamities that lay ahead. Everywhere around them, in the streets and even in the skies above, they saw warnings of impending danger.

4

LAUNCHING THE MAYFLOWER PROJECT

The Year of the Blazing Star

> Hung be the heavens with black, yield day to night!
> Comets, importing change of times and states,
> Brandish your crystal tresses in the sky.
>
> —SHAKESPEARE, *KING HENRY VI*
> *PART ONE* (1589–92)

An hour before dawn on 28 November, 1618, a physician looked up from his house on the northern edge of London and gazed over the city between the steeples and the chimneys. Above them, in the darkness to the southeast, he saw a blazing star. It was coloured a shade between green and blue, with a long white triangular tail. The comet gleamed with what he later called 'a bright resplendence'.

Medicine gave John Bainbridge a livelihood, but astronomy and mathematics excited him far more. An ambitious man of thirty-six, he believed in the ideas of Copernicus, and he read what Johannes Kepler wrote about the orbit of planets around the sun. In the comet he saw a chance to defend their findings. In the frost of early winter, Bainbridge tracked the apparition for four weeks, with the help of his 'telescopion, or trunkespectacle', one of the first in England. Peering through its lenses, he plotted the position of the star with a wooden cross-staff, collecting the data he needed to calculate its speed, altitude and distance from the earth. Day by day, he watched its colours fade and the comet diminish as it soared towards the northwest. He followed it past Scorpius and the Great Bear, until it veered away into oblivion beyond the Pole Star.

Swiftly the doctor completed a book about his observations. In the manner of its time it combined algebra, verse, and abject flattery of King James. Bainbridge pointed out that the gleaming star followed a course between New Guinea and the Arctic, and this could only mean one thing. As it travelled across the sky, the doctor said, the comet promised that God would reveal to the English the shining secret of another northwest passage, the icy route that led around the top of Canada, to reach the East Indies by way of the Pacific. In the star they beheld God's gift of wealth. From the Lord, the people of Great Britain would soon receive 'healthfull spices, precious Jewels, and Orientall riches', as Bainbridge put it in his most exalted prose.

Millions of others watched the comet too. From the Alps to Korea and from Iran to the Philippines we have vivid accounts of the blazing star, the brightest since the passing of Halley's comet eleven years before. A teenage student at Cambridge University looked out of a window during morning prayers, saw the comet, and thought its tail resembled a fox's brush. In China, observers called it a shining broom that swept across the heavens, while in Paris a journalist compared its round head to a burning coal, and its tail to a long sheaf of wheat. In Isfahan, the Spanish ambassador likened its green flame and its appearance each morning to the planet Venus. That year observers saw three comets, but everyone agreed that the emerald star was by far the most remarkable.

From his home in Austria, Kepler first saw it break through the clouds twenty-four hours after Bainbridge, and he carefully noted its features. In Rome the Jesuits had a professor of mathematics by the name of Orazio Grassi. He spoke of the crowds that gathered on hilltops to watch the visitation from the heavens, 'with no thought of sleep and no fear of the cold wind'. In Florence, bedridden by gout, or arthritis, or kidney stones, his rival the great Galileo received a long line of visitors, eager to exchange their impressions of the comet for his opinion, that it might be no more than vapour exhaled from the surface of the earth. Meanwhile a royal invalid, Anne of Denmark, King James's queen, lay sick with tuberculosis and dropsy. In the star the people of London saw a luminous warning of her end. Three months later, the queen was dead, and the Banqueting House of Whitehall Palace had burned to the ground.

Far to the west, another group of men and women stared at the blazing star with rapt attention. Astronomy fascinated the native people of America every bit as much as it enthralled the admirers of Galileo. Describing the natives he met in Connecticut in the 1630s, the English Puritan radical Roger Williams found that 'by occasion of their frequent lying in the fields or woods, they much observe the stars; and their very children can give names to many of them'. By the rising and the setting of the Pleiades, they constructed their calendar, fixing the best time to sow seed for corn, to plant beans, or to begin a hunting party. In their legends they gave events in the heavens a central role.

Beside Lake Huron, the Ojibwa still tell stories about a long-tailed climbing star that nearly ended life on earth long ago and one day will return to finish the task. In what is now the state of Maine, folklore collected among the Penobscot includes tales about a meteor that had warned of the outbreak of the American Civil War. We can be sure that the comet of 1618 caused just as much alarm in New England. Nearly forty years later, in a history of the colonies, Edward Johnson of Woburn, Massachusetts, described the way the people he called Indians followed the flaming star across the night sky. Like Bainbridge, they watched it each night for four weeks until it disappeared. 'They expected some strange things to follow,' Johnson said.

His laconic phrase conceals a world of meaning. The native people of New England split their cosmos into three realms: the sky, the earth, and a watery underworld. The boundaries between them could be crossed or penetrated by the souls of the dead, by a shaman in a trance, or by supernatural beings from above or below. Perhaps they thought of the comet as an eruption of divine power for good or ill from one cosmic zone into another. For men and women who prized the pattern of the heavens, an intervention of such a startling kind would foreshadow some great and unexpected event. Like the English expecting the death of a queen, most likely they made the comet an omen of destruction; and if they did, they were entirely correct.

According to Johnson, the comet prophesied not only the arrival of the *Mayflower*, bringing the light of salvation to the new continent, but also God's intervention to clear a space for his emissaries. 'A little before the removeall of that Church of Christ from Holland to Plimoth in New England, as the ancient Indians report,' Johnson wrote, 'there befell a great mortality.' By this, he meant a wave of epidemics, of smallpox, influenza, or hepatitis, carried on visiting ships, which began in 1616 and lasted for about three years, carving a demographic crater in the territory we now know as the northeastern United States.

Before the pestilence, about ten thousand native people may have lived in the southern half of Maine. Although these numbers are conjecture, as many as 90 per cent may have perished in the next two decades from sickness and in small wars. As for southern New England, before the epidemics the population may have numbered about ninety thousand. Again, maybe 90 per cent of them lost their lives.

Wherever it was seen, from the rivers of Maine to Manila and Beijing, the comet supplied the great sensation of the years before the *Mayflower* sailed. Connecting so many observers, from so many different cultures, with so many meanings latent in its path, the star was a social and political event, as well as a prodigy of nature. Every diplomat worth his expenses and every preacher worthy of a congregation found something to say about it. In the variety of their responses, and they were very diverse indeed, we see taking shape the complicated world from which the Pilgrims came.

On both sides of the Atlantic we have come to look upon the *Mayflower*, its voyage, and what followed as an entirely American story. We think of it simply in the light of what happened later, in the vast space between Quebec and California, making it solely a matter of American concern. This is an illusion: not a very damaging illusion, as illusions go, but an illusion nonetheless. The truth is that after the Pilgrims landed in America, on or near the boulder called Plymouth Rock, events on the western side of the Atlantic unfolded in intricate counterpoint with those taking place on the old side of the same ocean.

It was a complex fate to be a Calvinist in 1618, and faith did not bring tranquillity. William Bradford and the other *Mayflower* Pilgrims lived amid anxiety, phobia, and apocalyptic fantasy. They had obsessions entirely unlike our own, obsessions that the comet came to symbolise. We might prefer to think about the people of the time as men and women in our image, but if we do so, we run the risk of misunderstanding everything about them.

Of course, in their age we can find a long list of forerunners of modernity: not only the telescope, but also the invention or discovery of logarithms, newspapers, and the circulation of blood. Scientific navigation came into being, while the Dutch created a new system of global trade, linking China to Amsterdam by way of Brazil. And, as it happens, each of these innovations played their part in the origins of New England. And yet, if we wish to see things as they were, we have to recognise that an abyss of difference divides us from the Jacobean mind.

People did not believe that they stood on the cusp of something called the modern world. In Protestant Europe they were mostly frightened, alarmed and insecure, but for reasons bearing little likeness to our own nightmares. In the case of the Pilgrims, profound alarm gave birth to the project of migration, urging them to flee westward and to shun iniquity and defeat. As the comet appeared, Europe was approaching the great disaster called the Thirty Years' War: a war that the other side, the Roman Catholics, seemed all too likely to win.

Mother Courage and the **Mayflower**

When the comet first flew over London, the Pilgrims were trying to find the capital they needed for their plantation. Ten months earlier, they had obtained consent in principle from King James to settle within territory claimed by England in what were called 'the northern parts of Virginia', meaning modern New Jersey or New York State. From their base in Holland, the Pilgrims still had to find investors willing to fund their new colony until it became self-sufficient. As they tried each avenue, speculation about the comet surrounded them. At any time, a star so brilliant would arouse intense interest, but in 1618 the conditions guaranteed that it would call forth a multitude of interpretations. The year in question opened a dangerous phase in history.

The stargazing Doctor Bainbridge had no doubt that this was so. He was one of northern Europe's rare optimists, but his optimism took a sombre form. Schooled by Puritans, he was another ardent follower of John Calvin, he hated the Roman Catholic Church and the pope, and he longed to see them defeated. His reaction to the comet took two forms. One was a matter of physics, as Bainbridge tried to use the comet to prove that Copernicus and Kepler were correct about the solar system, but the other concerned theology. Bainbridge made the star a prophecy of doom for most men and women, and salvation for a few.

Bainbridge listed a spate of comets in the previous century, closely coinciding with the arrival of Martin Luther, and with other significant moments in the history of the Protestant Reformation that followed. For Bainbridge, the latest comet was an emblem of Providence in action, an omen of upheaval, a sign that God was working out some vast plan of destruction or redemption for mankind. It might even be a warning of the Second Coming of the Son of Man.

No human soul could say what horrors might precede the end, but in the thirteenth chapter of his Gospel, Saint Mark supplied a clue. Before Christ returned to judge mankind, his message must first be preached in all nations, the evangelist had said. Bainbridge reminded his readers that a blazing star appeared in 1606, the year before the English founded their first colony at Jamestown, Virginia, and this was a promise from God that he would shine the lamp of Protestant Christianity on the heathen people of the Americas. That accomplished, the way would lie open for retribution to fall on the wicked. The comet, said Bainbridge, spoke of the imminent destruction of the Roman Church, and then all men would face the Lord.

True, a few observers viewed the comet calmly, or doused forecasts such as this with cool skepticism. Grassi the scientific Jesuit disagreed with Galileo, arguing that the star was genuine and came from beyond the moon, but he also poured scorn on the Calvinists. He insisted that the star carried no theological lesson. Far away in London, James I agreed with him, dismissing the prophecies as nonsense. 'Concerning the blazing star,' wrote a contemporary, 'His Majesty ... swears it is nothing else but Venus with a firebrand in her arse.' The king composed some verses making the same point with his customary blend of learning and obscenity.

Elsewhere the prevailing mood was very different, and especially in Protestant Germany. There ministers preached scores of comet sermons. Many were published, and a few have survived, their brittle pages carrying pictures of the star soaring over rivers, towns and the sea. The words between the images conveyed a gloomy message, even darker than Bainbridge's. In the city of Magdeburg, a preacher spoke of the 'grosser und erschrecklicher Comet', the great and frightful comet, and he warned that God's sword of judgement might fall at any moment. At Ulm in

Bavaria, a pastor told his congregation that the blazing star spoke of famine, plague, war or earthquake, but as to which one it might be: 'That lies hidden with Dear God.'

In the Netherlands writers ventured specific prophecies, and they were grim too, dwelling again on the death of princes. Few believed that the gleaming object in the heavens warned of anything but bad news. Among the Dutch, the English ambassador was an industrious, clever man called Sir Dudley Carleton, who provided in his dispatches a detailed picture of the politics of his day. Even an envoy as shrewd as Carleton had little doubt that the comet conveyed a message in code from another dimension. For Carleton, it foretold the outbreak of a great European conflict. 'We shall have ... warres,' he wrote home, and he was right. As the comet appeared, the opening campaigns of the Thirty Years' War began between the Danube and the Elbe. On one side were Catholic Spain and Austria; on the other, the Protestant states of Bohemia and Germany.

We need not trace in detail the sequence of events; as for their horror, Bertolt Brecht portrayed the three decades of hostilities as amply as anyone could wish in his play *Mother Courage and Her Children*. But in parts of central Europe, the

percentage dead from violence, disease or famine
equaled the mortality rate from disease among the
natives of New England. At Magdeburg, where
the comet sermon had warned of a calamity, four-
fifths of the population failed to survive a long
siege.

Violence gathered momentum in the summer
before the star appeared. In May 1618, in the
episode known as the Defenestration of Prague,
the Bohemians rejected Hapsburg claims to
sovereignty over their country. At Prague Castle,
nationalists hurled through a window the only
local Catholics rash enough to defend the Austrian
position. When the Bohemians raised a militia to
repel an Austrian offensive, and began to threaten
Vienna itself, the Austrians turned to their friends
in Bavaria and Spain.

In August, Spanish troops seized the Valtelline
Pass. The main road over the Alps, it gave them a
safe supply line into the theatre of conflict. In
October, a palace revolution in Madrid brought
to power a new faction eager to intervene against
Bohemia. On 3 February, 1619, Philip III of
Spain committed his armies from the Low Coun-
tries and from Milan to the support of his allies.
With that, a local squabble became a continental
war between Roman Catholics and the Reformed,
while Protestant England and its own Dutch

Calvinist allies watched uneasily from the side-lines. A long truce between Spain and the Dutch Republic had only two years left to run, and in all likelihood the two old enemies would soon be at each other's throats again.

The fighting seemed certain to encompass all corners of the known world. Soon after the comet vanished, Carleton reported Dutch warnings that the Spanish navy was on the move. From Madrid, a fellow English diplomat sent word that the ships were bound for North Africa to put a stop to the pirates of Algiers. Others said that the fleet was heading for the Adriatic to seize Venetian bases, or to Genoa to land troops to be sent over the Valtelline. Or perhaps the Spanish intended to attack the Jamestown settlement.

Spain relied on her annual treasure fleet, bringing silver from Peru, and this might prompt her, Carleton warned, to make a preemptive strike against colonies that might be used as a base for Atlantic privateers. 'Our poore men in Virginia and the Barmudos' might be the target, said Carleton; but if his fears were justified, England could do little to fight back.

In 1618 she was an impotent country, beset by dangers of many kinds. There could be no better year for the Pilgrims to seek the king's permission for their own American colony. They found allies within the highest circle of the government at home, among men who recognised the need for patriotic volunteers.

The Principal Advancer

In the autumn of 1617, from their Dutch place of refuge, William Brewster and John Robinson had begun to send probing messages back across the North Sea as they planned a new life in the New World. The only existing English colony in America was the plantation at Jamestown, but the Virginia Company's royal charter gave it territorial rights over a vastly greater expanse of territory including the Hudson River area, close to modern New York, where the Leiden Pilgrims hoped to settle. For this they would require the Company's consent.

In the letters they sent to the Virginia Company, the Pilgrims played up their likeness to the French Huguenots with whom James I was on friendly terms. This was a sensible tactic, and it yielded results.

Brewster and Robinson had a friend in London called Sabine Staresmore, who acted as their agent. Staresmore belonged to a semi-secret congregation based in Southwark, south of the Thames, a twilight place where people did unofficial things. The congregation recruited tradesmen, apprentices, and many women, flirted with Separatism, and tried to avoid prosecution. Staresmore himself went to prison after the authorities raided an illegal gathering. But Jacobean London was a subtle and a complicated city. Despite his views, Staresmore obtained a meeting in February 1618 with one of the most senior men in the Virginia Company, a financier in his mid-fifties called Sir John Wolstenholme. Staresmore asked Wolstenholme to help the Pilgrims apply for the permission they needed from the company and from the Crown to settle in their territory, and to do so with a measure of religious freedom. Wolstenholme swiftly agreed to help.

A description of his meeting with Staresmore survives in William Bradford's history of the Plymouth Colony. Understandably, Bradford's narrative has always provided the backbone for books about the *Mayflower* Pilgrims. Later writers have often relied on it as pretty much their only source. But for all his qualities, Bradford left an incomplete account of events. We have to use the evidence from British archives to check, confirm and amplify what he wrote; if not, incidents such as the intervention by Wolstenholme simply lose their meaning.

Sir John was more than an average businessman, and the records that remain show that he had all manner of reasons to be cooperative. Although no evidence survives to suggest that he was a Puritan, Wolstenholme took his own Christianity very seriously. Near his country home at Stanmore, north of London, he built and endowed a new parish church. When he died, he left two hundred pounds for the repair of St Paul's Cathedral, ten times the annual wages of a highly skilled craftsman. Far from distrusting the Pilgrims, Sir John recommended them for a Virginia Company grant to pay for a school for Native American children.

Besides his piety, Sir John was a practical man – his few surviving papers contain a mass of detail about the prices of pepper, silk and indigo – and this would also make him listen sympathetically. Virginia badly needed new migrants, because fever had culled the number of settlers at Jamestown to about four hundred. Since Wolstenholme belonged to an inner clique of investors who made a monopoly profit by selling supplies to the colonists, he had an obvious incentive to encourage the Pilgrims to head westward. He was also something of a visionary and a patriot, worried by the fragile state of English commerce.

In business the English lagged far behind the Dutch. Allies they might be, but the Dutch were also fierce competitors. They made better cloth than the English, they controlled the herring fisheries of the North Sea, and they fought bloody skirmishes with English whalers in the Arctic. Perhaps five times the size of England's, their merchant marine consisted of bigger but cheaper vessels, manned lightly and hired by Amsterdam traders with far more capital than their counterparts in London. And in July 1617, word reached Whitehall Palace that the Dutch had found a new South American route to the East Indies by way of a channel avoiding Cape Horn. That autumn and winter, English diplomats sent home a stream of dispatches warning that England was falling behind its opponents everywhere.

From Paris, the English ambassador reported that the French intended to create 'a greate stocke and fleete for the undertakinge of remote trades, and particulerly to the West Indies.' A few weeks later, he heard that the merchants of Rouen and Dieppe were planning a whaling voyage to Greenland, flouting English claims to control the area. In Holland, Carleton used his network of agents to obtain the secret Dutch log of their discoveries in Patagonia, and he sent it back to Whitehall, only to learn that the king of Denmark was also fitting out ships for a voyage to the Spice Islands. With the French and Dutch doing business there too, said Carleton, 'the well will be drawne drie with so many buckets.'

In the opening months of 1618, the race for control of oceanic trade extended across the North Atlantic. In Paris, the French fur trader Samuel Champlain lobbied hard for royal support for his colony at Quebec. He asked Louis XIII for money and soldiers to help him find 'un chemin raccourcy pour aller à la Chine', a quick way to China, via the Great Lakes, and to ward off his English and Dutch rivals. As things turned out, the French Crown never threw its full weight behind him, but no one in London could be sure of that yet.

So, when Staresmore came to see him, Wolstenholme was busy with his own scheme to outflank Champlain and the Dutch. When a London author published the first English book on the mathematics of trigonometry, vital for navigation, he dedicated it to Sir John, describing Wolstenholme as one 'of the principall advancers of the Northwest discoverie', and indeed he was. Sir John was also a director of the East India Company, and in that role he sponsored voyages to the Canadian Arctic. Wolstenholme knew about the Dutch discovery in South America, and his response was to press ahead with yet another effort to find a shortcut to the Indies.

On 20 January, Sir John urged the East India Company to send a new expedition to Hudson Bay, offering to put up the bulk of the money. Meanwhile, he worked closely with a mathematician named Henry Briggs, another Cambridge man, a contemporary of John Robinson. Briggs had another theory, one that made it all the more important to secure the future of Virginia.

A Calvinist and a Puritan, Henry Briggs, like Robinson, had resigned his college fellowship during the purge of Puritans after King James first came to the throne. Briggs found a welcome in London from men of business, thanks to his own scientific expertise. He took the new tool called logarithms, first available in 1614, and showed mariners how to use them, combined with trigonometry, to calculate their course at sea. Like Bainbridge the astronomer, to whom he was close, Briggs dreamed of making England the mistress of the Indies. He believed that while a route to the Pacific must exist through Canada, they could also reach the same ocean from Virginia by way of a portage across the Appalachians.

Hence arose the need to plant more Englishmen in this essential region. By approaching Sir John, the Pilgrims had chosen the right man, and he did not disappoint them. Bradford mentions another revealing detail, easily missed but rich with significance. After seeing Staresmore, Wolstenholme hurried off to find a member of the king's Privy Council, the executive government of Jacobean England, to seek his support for the Pilgrim

project. The statesman in question was Fulke
Greville, the Chancellor of the Exchequer.

It would be hard to imagine a more willing
advocate for their cause. Under Queen Elizabeth,
Greville had served as treasurer of the navy, he
had Puritan sympathies, and since the 1580s he
had been an advocate of creating English Protestant
colonies in America. By 1618 he had reached a
peak of influence. He did so at a time when the
political environment suddenly made the Pilgrims
acceptable missionaries.

The Rigging of Ships

For the king, 1618 had begun in typical Jacobean
fashion, a mixture of high politics and farce,
drenched in alcohol. In January, it was reported
that James was indisposed, smitten with a sore toe,
from which the pain spread to his knee. He had
with him his favourite and lover, George Villiers,
a young man of twenty-five, recently created
Marquess of Buckingham. As he left the king's
bedchamber in the dark, Buckingham fell down
the stairs. He sprained his foot, vomited massively,
took to his own bed for fifteen hours, and then
hobbled about for several days with a stick.

Buckingham gave rise to scores of anecdotes,
but people wrote them down for reasons that were

entirely serious. At first he was merely an exquisite courtier, but during the course of 1618 he also became a forceful statesman. His every move and mishap attracted close attention. His rise to power occurred by way of a silent coup d'état at the start of the year, a changing of the guard that secured for Buckingham the ascendancy he maintained for the next decade. It also brought to the fore in London a circle of men, including Fulke Greville, who sympathised with the Pilgrims. Their motives were partly religious, but also a matter of grand strategy. They arose from economics, and from the urgent need to strengthen the Royal Navy.

For many years, James I had spent far more than the Crown received in revenue, staving off a crisis by selling assets. But by the end of 1617 the situation was becoming desperate. From the City of London, the king had borrowed the vast sum of £100,000, enough to build twenty of the largest English warships afloat. The money bled away, mostly to pay for a royal tour of Scotland, and the City refused to lend more. The episode wrecked the credit rating of the Crown. Only one option remained, a marriage between his son Prince Charles and a Spanish princess, the Infanta, in return for a handsome dowry, but Spain knew that it held the upper hand. No swift agreement

seemed likely. As the marriage negotiations floun-
dered, the king at last accepted the need for
financial reform.

James promoted a group of new, efficient men,
allied with Buckingham, to cut expenditure and
find new ways to raise money. Commissioners
began to attack extravagance in the royal household,
but if they were to make lasting improvements,
they had to deal with the navy. Blighted by corrup-
tion, the fleet consumed far more cash than any
other service, but it was ill equipped and poorly
manned, barely capable of leaving harbour.

Change was required, and not only for fiscal
reasons. Nearly a year before the comet, reports
had already reached London of naval rearmament
in Spain. Added to that was the new threat from
the pirates of North Africa. They had begun to raid
outward into the Atlantic, attacking English fishing
vessels, taking their crews hostage, and demanding
ransom. At Alicante, three English merchant ships
found themselves fighting off a forty-strong Arab
fleet, while more pirates were sighted only sixty
miles from the coast of Cornwall.

Sooner or later, England would have to mount
a punitive foray against Algiers, but its ability to
do so was doubtful. So, in 1618, Buckingham
persuaded King James to make him lord admiral.
Commissioners began to investigate the fleet,

swiftly uncovering evidence of waste and embezzlement. Wolstenholme served on the naval commission, while Fulke Greville oversaw the process from his post at the Treasury. In the circumstances of the time, they had a further motive to encourage the Pilgrims, and again it was a matter of maritime concern.

Greville belonged to the anti-Spanish party at court. They were men who hoped to revive English sea power and to repeat the victories of Sir Francis Drake. His closest colleague of all was Buckingham's naval mentor, Sir John Coke, a man fascinated by warship design and logistics. Among the finest archives from the period are Coke's papers, listing the navy's requirements in intricate detail. A strong navy needed naval stores – 'sea-arsenals', said Greville, and dockyards filled with 'ordnance, pitch, rosin, tar, masts, deal-boards, cordage' – and Coke itemised their quantities and cost in long memoranda. Hence the importance of establishing a new colony in the northern parts of Virginia or in the Hudson Valley, which contained these commodities in abundance. The same year Captain John Smith, the Jamestown colonist and explorer, shot off one of many letters, urging the Privy Council towards New England, as a source for 'all things belonging to the building and rigging of Shippes'.

Coke and Greville shared another colleague, a man whose name leaps from the pages of the Pilgrim narratives. William Bradford singled out for gratitude a politician, Sir Robert Naunton. It was Naunton, according to the Pilgrims, who convinced the king that the Pilgrims were harmless, however much they might want liberty of conscience. It would cost him nothing to let them go, since the Pilgrims would pay their own way by fishing, Naunton said. This gave the king a chance to be witty. 'So God have my soul,' James replied. ''Tis an honest trade;'twas the Apostles' own calling.'

We have no reason to doubt that this conversation occurred. It was exactly the kind of remark that James made, and in 1618 Naunton bathed in the glow of royal approval. Another loyal adherent of Buckingham, in January he became joint secretary of state, very nearly the highest rank within the government. Naunton saw all England's diplomatic papers, he headed its secret service, he loathed the Spaniards, he feared Dutch rivalry, and he was a close friend of Greville. We need look no further for his motives for helping the Pilgrims. Without bases in America, England could not challenge Spanish control of the western ocean. And without the supplies New England might provide, the Royal Navy could not put to sea. For

Naunton, most likely it was all a matter of politics and naval doctrine, with Calvinism adding the impetus of zeal.

Naunton and Greville were on the same side as the Pilgrims, but of course Brewster and his colleagues were not merely tools of the English state. Even if they had been, an insolvent monarchy could not help them with hard cash. As it was, thanks partly to factional squabbles inside the Virginia Company, even after royal approval it took nearly two years and two attempts for the Pilgrims to obtain the definitive patent allowing them to settle in the company's territory. For funds they had to rely on young, untried investors from London, with little capital between them.

Raising the Money

According to the Jamestown veteran Captain John Smith, the finance for the Mayflower Project came from a consortium of seventy investors, a mixed bag of gentlemen, merchants and tradesmen. When Smith's descriptions of people and events are checked against other sources they mostly tend to confirm his reliability, and so they do on this occasion.

We know the names of forty-six of the *Mayflower* financiers, most of them contained in a letter dated

1626, which William Bradford transcribed and copied into his history of the Plymouth Colony. From information preserved elsewhere, we can establish the origins or occupations of at least eighteen. A handful, perhaps no more than three or four, were religious radicals like the Separatists. The rest of the investors were either mainstream Puritans or men with no pious enthusiasm either way, for whom the *Mayflower* was strictly business.

None of them appear to have had any prior experience of investing in voyages to North America. In 1620 the Virginia Company made a list of its own shareholders, and no overlap exists with Bradford's list of names. Nor were any of the *Mayflower* investors involved in the East India Company which traded for silk and spices in Asia. Typically the *Mayflower* investors were London-based businessmen at early stages of their careers, young and ambitious but with only a small amount of money to spare. Chiefly they operated in the woollen textile trade, England's principal industry other than farming and its only substantial source of exports to continental Europe.

Investing in the *Mayflower* was always going to be a high risk venture. In its early years, the Plymouth Colony ran up heavy losses as it struggled to survive. By the time it broke even financially in 1628, only six of the initial seventy backers remained. The rest had long since died, withdrawn or sold out. However, the original *Mayflower* concept had not been rash or commercially unsound. In North America the investors expected to find vast new supplies of commodities that they could sell at home in England at a handsome profit. Although, as things turned out, the *Mayflower* colonists never sent back to London very much by way of the naval stores that John Smith had described – tar and pitch and masts and so on – they did find another, far more valuable item, the fur of the North American beaver.

The fur trade would prove to be the saviour of the *Mayflower* settlers. From beaver skins, craftsmen made the smooth, sleek and tactile felt that could be shaped into expensive beaver hats, one of the most sought-after fashion accessories of the sixteenth and seventeenth centuries. In the 1570s, when beaver hats first came into vogue in Paris, the fur to make the felt had come only from Russia, but in the 1580s French seafarers had begun to find new sources of beaver skins in the great river valleys of North America. The Dutch followed, trading for furs with native people up and down the American coast. However, until the 1610s the English hat-makers continued to rely on Russian beaver skins from Siberia, which they bought in the White Sea port of Archangel. But the Arctic voyage to Archangel was dangerous and the Tsarist regime charged high prices not only for beaver fur but also for the raw materials for rope. At last, in the summer of 1620, English merchants began to look across the Atlantic for a better alternative. As the Virginia Company put it in a promotional pamphlet which it issued in June, 'the rich furs ... and cordage, which we draw from Russia with so great difficulty, are to be had in Virginia and the parts adjoining with ease and plenty'.

Here was the business case for the voyage of the *Mayflower*. It made perfect sense to look to North America for new sources of profit at a time when, for a young entrepreneur in London, the business outlook at home was very bleak. In seventeenth-century England, land was still by far the most important form of investment; but, after many decades of steeply rising rents for rural property, the price of real estate had risen to so high a level that future returns were going to be poor. In 1619 and 1620 the woollen export trade was also sinking into a slump, caused by the onset of the Thirty Years' War.

The best opportunities lay in the luxury market, where there were handsome profits to be made by importing not only Asian spices and silks but also French and Spanish wines, olive oil and much else that could be sold at high margins to the wealthy. But this required capital and connections. In practice a small mercantile elite – men like Sir John Wolstenholme – controlled the most lucrative luxury trades. Young entrepreneurs like the *Mayflower* investors were hemmed in and trapped, unable to compete with monopolies and rackets, such as the East India Company, which controlled the economy's commanding heights.

Risky though it was, the Mayflower Project offered its investors a chance to break free from London's commercial confines. Despite the inroads made by the French and the Dutch, neither country had yet established a stranglehold over the transatlantic fur trade, and there were sections of the American coast that appeared to be wide open. Even so the project was going to require strong nerves, and some of the men involved were going to be the sort of people who always try to cut corners. This was certainly true of the *Mayflower* consortium's leader, Thomas Weston.

Aged thirty-six in 1620, Weston had no Puritan ideals of his own. In fact, the scanty evidence available suggests that he was raised a Roman Catholic. However, he had every commercial motive to want to try his luck with an American venture. Weston made a precarious living trading in woollens and haberdashery between England and the Netherlands, but as the textile trade began to dwindle his business collapsed. And so he reached out to a long-standing contact, a London haberdasher named Edward Pickering who also had a retail outlet in Amsterdam. Pickering was a Separatist and he knew and actively supported the Leiden Pilgrim congregation. In the spring and summer of 1620, Weston and Pickering recruited the rest of the *Mayflower* investors.

In the years that followed, William Bradford and his Pilgrim comrades came to regard Thomas Weston as a rogue who very nearly wrecked the Plymouth Colony with his underhand dealings. He certainly insisted that the colony should be a commercial enterprise as well as a mission inspired by religious ideals.

Far from being a commune, the *Mayflower* colony was legally constituted as a joint stock company, chiefly financed by Weston's consortium. Its purpose, in the words of Weston's contract with the settlers, was to make a profit from 'trade, traffic, trucking, working and fishing'. The company would own all the settlers' land, their tools, their livestock and all the profits, should any materialise. After seven years, the company would be wound up and its assets would be divided out between the shareholders in proportion to the capital each one had invested. Among the *Mayflower* passengers, some invested money of their own alongside the consortium. Those who had no capital, but simply came on the ship, were each deemed to have a single share. It was a hard bargain, and it was to grow still harder as the summer of 1620 wore on and the date for departure to America drew nearer.

In the fourth week of July, the English Separatist contingent from Leiden set off from the Dutch harbour of Delftshaven, travelling on a small ship, the *Speedwell*. She was to sail to Southampton to rendezvous with the larger ship Thomas Weston had hired, the *Mayflower* of London. The two ships would load their supplies and remaining passengers and then set off across the Atlantic. On board the *Speedwell* the Separatists were led by their wealthiest man, John Carver, who had married the preacher John Robinson's sister-in-law.

On arrival at Southampton, Carver and his comrades met Thomas Weston but the atmosphere was fraught and bad-tempered. Weston's money had been slow to arrive. To reduce the influence of the Separatists, his fellow investors insisted on sending their own man, Christopher Martin, a Puritan merchant from Essex, to act as the colony's governor. He was also the expedition's supply officer, purchasing provisions but quarrelling with

John Carver about their cost and where to buy them.

Christopher Martin would die during the first winter in America, removing one potential source of division and dissent within the colony. But the difficulties with Thomas Weston grew steadily worse. Before returning to London, where he remained for two more years before sailing to America himself in 1622, Weston inserted a new and onerous clause in the contract with the settlers. He insisted that in the New World the colonists should work seven days a week for the company. Even their houses would be treated as company assets to be divided up when the seven years were over.

This clause of the contract could never be enforced, and by 1627 Thomas Weston had long since vanished from the scene. But it was an omen of trouble to come. Short of supplies, because their own money had run out, the passengers on the *Mayflower* and the *Speedwell* urgently needed to get across the Atlantic as soon as possible. The voyage was likely to take at least eight weeks; which meant that if they were to reach America with time to spare to build a settlement before winter set in, they had to leave England no later than the middle of August.

At first, the journey appeared to be going according to plan. On 5 August, the *Mayflower* and the *Speedwell* set off from Southampton; but then the *Speedwell* sprang a leak and began to fill with water. Both ships put in to Dartmouth, the *Speedwell* underwent repairs, and off they went once more. They had already passed Land's End and sailed 300 miles into the Atlantic when the same thing happened again. This time the unseaworthy *Speedwell* limped back to Plymouth with the *Mayflower* at her side. The *Speedwell* was discharged and sent home, and the *Mayflower* made ready to set out for America alone.

She was already an ageing ship, nearing the end of the usual working life of fifteen years for a merchant vessel of her type. Built for the wine trade with France and Spain, the *Mayflower* had a volume of 180 tons. Each ton represented the space required to hold a cask full of claret or sherry. She measured roughly one hundred feet long, from the beak of her prow to the hindmost tip of her superstructure. Amidships she was roughly twenty-five wide, and she carried artillery to defend herself against the pirates from Algiers.

The *Mayflower*'s master was an experienced, prosperous London-based mariner by the name of Christopher Jones. No record survives to show that he had ever crossed the Atlantic before. It was September 1620; the war in Europe was proving to be disastrous for the Protestant cause; and the slump in the English textile trade had turned into a deep depression which blighted the entire economy. On board the *Mayflower*, Mr Jones carried as passengers a human cargo of 102 men, women and children.

About half of them came from the Separatist community in Leiden, while the rest were an assortment of farmers, tradesmen and labourers whose religious views and motives for the voyage are mostly unknown. Fewer than fifty of the passengers were adult males. Jones's crew numbered at least nineteen men, and possibly as many as thirty. On his overcrowded ship, Christopher Jones made his final preparations for what would have to be his last attempt at the ocean crossing. It was now very late in the year.

5

THE SHIP AND HER MASTER

The Mayflower in Plymouth Sound

Plymouth is generally considered, and not
without good reason, as the most capacious and
secure rendez-vous in Great Britain.

—SAILING DIRECTIONS FOR SHIPS OF
THE ROYAL NAVY, FIRST HALF
OF THE NINETEENTH CENTURY

On Wednesday, 6 September, a brisk wind blew
over the sea outside the entrance to the sound. It
came from the direction of an island, the Mewstone,
a green pyramid of rock that leaps up from the
waves like a small wet Matterhorn, situated offshore
to the east. A *Mayflower* passenger called the wind
'a fine small gale', and it carried the ship rapidly
into the English Channel and towards the Atlantic.
As Christopher Jones took her out of the haven
on her way towards America, on her starboard

side the *Mayflower* passed a headland, facing the
Mewstone across four miles of water. Made of
slate dotted with quartz, and topped with grass
and yellow furze, Penlee Point dips and tumbles
from a height of three hundred feet down into
the sea.

When tankers or frigates enter or leave the
approaches to Plymouth, they should keep the
grey cliffs of Penlee half a mile away. At the foot
of the promontory, crags spill out along the seabed
to form a reef. At low tide the waves cover the
Draystone, as it is known, to a depth of only one
fathom. Fishermen will tell you that conger eels
dwell within its crevices, waiting to bite the
unwary who find them in their nets. The reef has
killed seamen in their thousands. The approaches
to Plymouth contain many hazards, with ancient
names – the Panther, the Tinker, and the wicked
little Shagstone, tiny, square, rising out of the
water opposite Penlee – and mariners must know
them all.

So it is along much of the rest of the coast on
the way out to the west, where spurs of uneroded
rock jut into the sea to form dangerous headlands.
A chain of them extends as far as the Lizard
Peninsula, the last English landmark before
America and the most dangerous promontory of
them all. In Jones's day mariners faced their greatest

risks on the trip home, when they sometimes fatally mistook it for Ushant, one hundred miles to the south at the tip of France. So, the year before the *Mayflower* sailed, a Cornish squire built the first lighthouse on the Lizard.

'The subtilnes of the tide imbayeth ships without prevention,' said Sir John Killigrew, as he described the perils of the shore, hoping to take fees from Dutch shipowners tired of losing vessels sailing back from the East Indies. The *Mayflower* may have been one of the first ships to see his winking candles. Four years earlier, another lighthouse had appeared at Dungeness, at the entrance to the Strait of Dover, and these were the first of their kind since Roman lights cast their beams over the channel many centuries before. The Jacobean revival of lighthouses was a sign that times were changing. So too was the voyage of the *Mayflower*, a venture forming part of England's emergence as a great maritime power.

English enterprise by sea was about to undergo a metamorphosis. Until the 1620s, more than a century after the foundation of New Spain, English skippers still remained scarce in the waters off the mainland of North America. In 1619, only six English ships made fishing voyages to the Gulf of Maine. For cod, Newfoundland still reigned supreme. The customs records list only one ship leaving the

Thames that year for Jamestown, the *Bona Nova*, with a hundred settlers and a jumbled cargo of shoes, boots, hoes, and assorted ironmongery.

Only eight English ships altogether sailed to Virginia in 1619. The colony there still had little to offer by way of business, since the tobacco leaf sent home each season came to little more than fifty tons, barely enough to fill a large fishing boat. And yet by the end of the next decade, the bias of sea traffic began to change profoundly, and the passage to America at last became routine. By the middle of the 1630s, forty ships each year were leaving the port of London for Chesapeake Bay or New England. Soon each of the leading harbours in Devon had four or five master mariners who made regular crossings.

The voyages travelled by English merchant ships fell into a new pattern, tilted westward. New England owed its origins to this maritime change of direction. However zealous Puritans might be, they needed sea captains willing and able to take them westward, and money to pay for the journey. Once on the other side, they had to service their debts and pay for essential items from the old country: the goods carried by the *Bona Nova*, but also glass, paper, lead, copper, Sheffield knives and hatchets, gunpowder and firearms, and most of all livestock. Alongside the beaver, and Puritans, imported cattle were the mammals that made Massachusetts what it became. Ships were needed too, more ships and bigger ships with ample hulls for carrying heifers as well as Pilgrims. Until they were available, nobody could build in New England a city on a hill.

It had to be possible to cross the North Atlantic in both directions more swiftly and more safely than in the past: in *both* directions, because to investors and indebted settlers the return journey mattered as much as the voyage out. Feasibility required experiment, and speculation. In the first thirty years of the seventeenth century, innovations such as Killigrew's lighthouse began to transform English navigation. Without this process, much of it by trial and error, Puritan America could not have come into being in the way in which it did.

Just as wind and tide converge around Penlee into a vortex of waters, but a swirl with a pattern beneath it, so a new turbine of connections began to drive events in the North Atlantic, spun in motion by new flows of trade and people across the ocean. Of all this, the *Mayflower* and Christopher Jones were physical symbols. At first sight, we seem to know little about Jones: merely the crude, random data of two weddings, nine baptisms of his children, his burial, and his lawsuits. Look a little deeper, and we find that we can reconstruct his career and the

English maritime world that he inhabited on the eve of the founding of the British Empire.

The Life and Times of Christopher Jones

Christopher Jones was born in about 1570 in the port of Harwich, on the eastern coast of England. Queen Elizabeth called Harwich 'a pretty town', and to her it was intensely loyal, sending three ships to join Drake against the Armada. Local seamen caught lobsters, fished for cod as far away as Iceland, or carried coal from Newcastle to London. Like Plymouth, Harwich had grown wealthier still by pillaging Spanish ships, though the business it did best was to export English woollen cloth to be dyed and finished in Holland. A boy raised there would also hear stories told by explorers. When Jones was eight or so, Harwich men sailed to Baffin Island in the Canadian Arctic.

Pretty or not, Harwich possessed characteristics that made it ideal for the training of a seafarer. Thanks to the winds and currents of the North Sea, and thanks to the silt that drifted down the coast, the entrance to Harwich contained dangerous sandbanks, with names such as the Pies, the Pole Head, and the Platters. To the north was the long pebble spit of Orford Ness, where on a single night in 1627 a storm wrecked more than thirty ships. In these testing waters Jones served his apprenticeship. His father and his stepfather were both Harwich skippers, and at eighteen Jones inherited his first part share of a ship.

He belonged to a clique of mariners and shipwrights who governed the town with harsh discipline. They sentenced five women to hang as witches in 1605, while harlots were dragged through the streets on a cart, and dice games were banned. Harwich resembled other seaports around the English coast, from Hull in the north to Barnstaple in the west, where sea captains and merchants ran local government, levying municipal taxes to pay for street cleaning, jails, and parish constables. They formed part of an international circuit of little marine republics, from the Baltic to the Pyrenees, Calvinist by inclination, from Gdansk in modern Poland to La Rochelle in southwestern France. In America, when New Plymouth and New Boston reached maturity, they formed the western extension of the same network, tossed across the ocean like the end of a coil of rope.

In his mid-thirties Jones became an oligarch himself, named as a burgess of Harwich in a new charter granted by King James. He also built a ship of his own, the *Josian*, named after his second wife. At 240 tons, the craft was larger than average. She must have cost around a thousand pounds, a sizable sum when a ship's master hired by a merchant earned no more than fifty pounds a year, and Jones used her for trading voyages as far south as Bordeaux. Then, in 1611, he became one of a group of Harwich men who outgrew the town and moved south to the Thames. Jones made his new home at Rotherhithe, a mile downstream from the Tower of London.

By that time, he had swapped the *Josian* for a quarter share in the smaller *Mayflower*, and narrowly escaped disaster in the North Sea. In 1609, he guided her safely back from Norway through 'an extraordinary great storm', with a cargo of timber, tar and fish. As a crew member later recalled, in an effort to save the ship Jones dumped over the side a hundred planks of wood. Many weeks later they struggled back home, only to find that the man who owned the tar, wood and rotting herring was bankrupt, unable to pay for them. When he moved to the capital, Jones found a safer, more regular trade. He also followed the tide of history.

Before the 1590s, Rotherhithe and Ratcliff were country retreats, places where Londoners hunted deer and rabbits. Suddenly, as the wealth and the population of London grew, they began to fill with new houses for mariners, with alongside them abattoirs, inns, and England's first sugar refinery. In the late 1620s, a census counted nearly 120 master mariners in these two parishes alone. Excavations in the year 2000 found traces left behind by these new Jacobean citizens, immense quantities of imported pottery, Venetian glass, and some of the earliest clay tobacco pipes uncovered in England. The same archaeology also unearthed some of England's first glass wine bottles, designed to be packed into crates.

Wine flowed like the Thames through the commercial veins of London. It made the fortune of the mariners of Rotherhithe. Jones's most affluent neighbour was another ship's master, named Anthony Wood, skipper of the *Rainbow*, who ranked above Jones at the very top of the parish list of taxpayers, owner of shares in three ships and a portfolio of houses on both sides of the river. Wood was another visitor to Plymouth in the autumn of 1620, sailing out of the Sound in October for Alicante, and he owed his wealth to the excellent vintages that the Spanish port supplied. Alicante was the favourite drink of King James himself. A pint of it cost sixpence, close to a labourer's daily wage, and the trade was very lucrative indeed.

The largest client of Christopher Jones was one William Speight. He lived in London's Vintry Ward, the wine merchants' district, opposite the

Globe Theatre. After buying his wine wholesale in France, shipping it home, and paying all his costs, Speight could clear six pounds of profit per ton. In May 1620, Jones and the *Mayflower* sailed back into the Thames on their last trip before carrying the Pilgrims. He carried fifty tons of wine for Speight, enough to make Speight as much money as ten English clergymen earned in a year. Holding the rank of warden of the Company of Merchant Taylors, Speight owned country estates in Suffolk and tenements, shops, cellars and warehouses in the City. At his death in 1621 he left a string of bequests to schools and the inmates of prisons, the charities supported most often by London's mercantile elite.

Men like Speight, Wood and Jones prospered because of a surge in the intake of alcohol as the income of the landowning classes grew. At the peak of the wine trade, in 1615, London imported nearly three times as much wine as it had in a typical year twenty years previously. English customers were not only drinking more but also paying more for what they drank: during the same two decades, at La Rochelle the price of white wine doubled. Taste became more subtle too, as the English widened their horizons from claret to Sauternes, Spanish sweet wines, and brandy. The first hard liquor from Cognac arrived in London in about 1560, most likely rough stuff, like an Italian grappa, but during the reign of King James the Dutch refined it and made it an item of choice. A typical Jones voyage in 1615 saw the *Mayflower* bring back from France eighty tons of the new spirit. She carried to New England at least one keg of French or Dutch eau-de-vie.

When wine ships sailed back and forth, they did more than simply fill the wallet of a William Speight. Their voyages made the Protestant maritime network deeper and tighter, binding it together with exchanges of men, women, and ideas. By the 1620s, each leading French haven along the Atlantic coast had a solid community of English and Scottish traders and brokers, with Dutchmen in still larger numbers. At the centre of the web lay the city of La Rochelle, the Huguenot bastion that tied together the long loops of commerce from north to south, and from the Levant to Newfoundland.

Down from the Baltic came grain, hemp and tar, to be sold to the French or shipped on to Spain. Back up from the Mediterranean and Gascony came currants from Greece and Turkey, iron from Galicia, and Spanish colonial goods, tobacco, or raw sugar. Along the coast to the south of La Rochelle lay immense salt marshes and the fortified port of Brouage. English ships bound back

from the Grand Banks could sell their cod to fish-
eating Catholics and then fill their empty holds
with French salt for packing their next consignment. Or they, and the Dutch, would simply carry
it back home: overcast northern nations had no
salt pans to rival those of southwestern France. In
an age of sail, the French made the best canvas,
and this too could be purchased at La Rochelle.
There the English also found allies. The Huguenots
had their own *armée navale*, fifteen warships ready
to fight the French king.

Jones and the *Mayflower* found a place within
this pattern of trade, but like the commerce with
the East Indies it carried no guarantee of success.
Everything, including the fortune made by
William Speight, depended on finding ready takers
for the only currency that London's merchants
possessed. England had no gold or silver mines,
and it was strictly illegal to export coin or precious
metals without a license from the Privy Council.
The country's meagre stocks of bullion were
mostly earmarked to pay for the silk and spices
returning from Asia. So when the *Mayflower* left
London for France, her hold was crammed with
English woollens, the nation's only substantial
export. Instead of cash, Speight and his rivals used
thousands of yards of raw cloth to pay for French
or Spanish wine.

Woollen textiles were England's strength, but also a source of vulnerability. If anything happened to deter the buyers in Europe and cloth failed to sell, the way of life of mariners such as Jones would swiftly disintegrate. A family man, Jones had to fill his ship and keep her busy. In 1620 this was rapidly becoming far more difficult than in the past.

In June, as Jones was hired to cross the Atlantic, expert observers in London had already seen the warning signs that the economy was slumping into a dangerous decline. In Devon too, life was becoming more complicated, at sea and on land alike, for merchants, for fishermen, and for the soldiers in the fort at Plymouth. New problems had to be solved. As yet, very few men and women believed that the mainland of North America provided the answers.

Diverse Friends There Dwelling

On 6 September, as she put out towards the Atlantic, the *Mayflower* must have passed a fishing boat called the *Covenant*. In September, listed in the records of the port, the fishing fleet from Newfoundland came hurrying home to Plymouth, sixty-five vessels in all, travelling in convoy eight at a time. In 1620 the *Covenant* made it back first, on the very day on which the *Mayflower* left for America.

At thirty tons, the *Covenant* was small. In this, she was typical of the craft that sailed to Newfoundland. Only seven of the town's Newfoundland vessels had a volume of a hundred tons or above, and none came anywhere near the *Mayflower*'s size. For this reason, cod fishing alone could never form the basis of permanent English colonies on the American mainland. The ships employed simply did not have the capacity required. Few of the Newfoundland boats could carry more livestock than a few goats or pigs.

Cod fishing yielded a good return even if the ships were small, and that was the problem. Dried and salted, the fish conveyed in the *Covenant* would fetch three hundred pounds on a Spanish quayside. And train oil, squeezed from cod, walruses or whales, added another stream of profit. Used to make soap for washing newly woven cloth, it sold for only twopence a pint, but it came back in batches of more than a thousand gallons per boat. Plymouth men had begun to sail to Newfoundland as long ago as the 1540s, but the cod voyages were closed circuits that did not lead elsewhere. As long as the Newfoundland trade continued to thrive, and while woollens could be bartered for wine, merchants had no need to think about mainland America. Five years before, Captain John Smith had returned to Devon from Monhegan Island, nine miles off the coast of Maine, bouncing with enthusiasm for the country he named New England. He did not find an eager reception.

Written up in a book published in 1616, his chart and his tales of Cape Cod, fish, fur and timber failed to arouse excitement. Dashing and eloquent, John Smith did his best, touring the western ports to promote the opportunities that he had seen. Few wished to follow him, and no colonists willingly did. Later, Smith listed twenty-two voyages to New England between 1614 and 1618, from London or from Devon. They included landings on the Cape, but no one tried to found a settlement.

Three days' sail from Boston, Monhegan remained the favoured destination, as a fishing or a trading post, but it could not host a colony: the rocky island measured little more than a mile long. Smith had also visited a place to the south called Accomack. He named it New Plymouth on his chart, speaking of its 'excellent good harbour' and 'good land', but nobody took much notice. After reading his narrative, the *Mayflower* Pilgrims aimed elsewhere, for New York Harbour, recently visited by an old shipmate of Smith's. He had sailed around Long Island and sent a report home, suggesting like Henry Briggs that the Hudson offered a route to the Pacific.

Nevertheless, although few people had grasped the point, times were changing and gradually making New England more compelling. Sometimes, cod became scarce off the Grand Banks, or disappeared entirely for a season. This happened in 1621, encouraging some adventurous traders to think again about Maine and Massachusetts. The cod voyages also became more dangerous, thanks to the pirates from North Africa.

They ambushed the fishing boats on the way home, because they were too small and lightly armed to put up a fight. In the years that followed, the pirates took at least seven thousand English sailors captive, about half of them from Devon, and in due course this helped to feed Puritan discontent with the Crown. And, once again, we find the Dutch closing in to undermine England's business. Dominating the herring grounds of the North Sea, the Dutch had mostly left Newfoundland alone. Until, that is, the year of the comet, when they began to sail to 'Terra Nova', as they called it, challenging the English in their old domain.

Jones and the Pilgrims would have heard talk about matters such as these at Plymouth. Later, when the Pilgrims came to narrate their adventures, they included a typically cryptic allusion to the place. At Plymouth, they said, they were kindly entertained 'by divers friends there dwelling'. Who were the friends in question? The Pilgrims do not say, but two likely candidates present themselves. In their different ways, both men were looking for alternatives across the ocean. Their careers add another layer of explanation for the leap across the Atlantic that would soon occur.

The first man was the Plymouth postmaster, Abraham Jennings. He was in his early forties, and he owned a quay in the centre of the waterfront. As a young man, Jennings had supplied iron pots, locks and other bits and pieces to the first Englishmen who tried to settle in New England, the failed Popham Colony of 1607, at Fort St George in Maine. Then he apparently forgot about the New World, until the new circumstances of the 1620s aroused his interest once more.

Until then, Jennings stuck to the familiar. Dealing in cod, figs and raisins, he bought wine from the Canaries, or shipped merchandise back from Alicante. Then suddenly, in 1622, he begins to reappear in records relating to North America. A little later, Jennings bought control of Monhegan. He started to bring back beaver pelts, nine hundred in 1626, a type of cargo new to Plymouth. For some reason, he soon tired of the venture and sold the island, but his involvement was a landmark. For the first time since the Popham debacle, a substantial Devon merchant, rooted in the older European trades, had invested capital in the territory north of the Potomac. He did so in alliance with a second man, who had other reasons to look westward.

To find him, the Pilgrims would have to climb up to Plymouth Fort and ask for the governor. Nobody in the realm, besides John Smith, thought more about New England than Sir Ferdinando Gorges. The fort's commander, he came from an old French family from Normandy. His fascination with America appears to have arisen entirely from patriotism, and curiosity. He seems never to have made a penny from his efforts.

At fifty-four, Gorges had been fascinated by America for more than a decade. His obsession dated back to 1605, when he met three Abenaki native people, shipped back to Plymouth by an early English voyager to Maine. Gorges questioned them closely about their home, and most of all about its rivers leading far inland. Excited by what he heard, Gorges helped lead the creation in 1607 of the Plymouth Company, designed to operate north of the Delaware, as a twin of the London company that founded Jamestown to the south. It planted the Popham Colony, and then it backed John Smith's voyage of 1615. Beyond that, it achieved nothing, but Gorges refused to give up.

As the *Mayflower* prepared to sail, Sir Ferdinando was about to relaunch the company, with a new name and a new royal charter. The Council for New England came into being on 3 November. Packed with marquesses, earls and a clergyman or two, in the name of His Majesty it held dominion over all the land and sea between the fortieth parallel and the forty-eighth, from the St Lawrence to the site of Philadelphia, and as far west as the Pacific.

Because it later became extinct, abolished by King Charles, and because its papers mostly vanished, the council has never commanded much respect. Historians in America often portray the council and its creator as absurd feudal relics, intent on turning New England into an aristocratic fiefdom. Up to a point this is fair. Gorges antagonised many people, especially the fishermen of Devon, by charging fees for licenses to look for American bass and cod. But Gorges was no fool, and far from being narrow-minded he was another visionary of a kind.

Much later, he fell out with the Puritans of Massachusetts, but to begin with he happily welcomed the Pilgrims as settlers, speaking highly of their good relations with the native people whom they met. He recruited merchants as partners, inviting Jennings to join the council. Far earlier than other men, Sir Ferdinando saw the need to build much bigger ships to service the new colonies, to be paid for, he hoped, with a loan from the East India Company. If he charged fees for fishing, it was because he needed to defend the Gulf of Maine against the Spanish, the French, or the Dutch.

In 1621, Gorges made his own disappointing tour of England's west country, looking for colonists to follow the Pilgrims. He aroused as little interest as John Smith. Gorges spoke in the military language of empire, and perhaps this deterred investors. Security had to come first, he said, as he listed his American priorities: 'erecting forts, placeing of Garrisons, maynteyninge shipps of warr upon the Coasts, and officers for the more safe and absolute Government of those parts'. Gorges had militarised Plymouth Sound, with cannon protecting each strongpoint. Now he wished to make the North Atlantic a fortified English lake, with Virginia and New England as the armed bulwarks of a new empire.

Like most of his fellow countrymen, Sir Ferdinando believed that another war with Spain was unavoidable. At Plymouth he stood in the front line. We can imagine him, pacing up and down his parapet, watching the *Mayflower* come and go, fuming at the politicians who withheld the funds he needed to man the fort and fight the pirates, and cursing the merchants who failed to share his vision of western adventure. For the time being, however, failure seemed the most likely outcome in a commercial project of any kind.

Damp and Deadness

Over the early years of the Plymouth Colony hung the shadow of the economic depression of the early 1620s. The voyage of the *Mayflower* took place at the moment when unease about the economy crystallised into acute alarm. Capital was scarce, and demand collapsed. Tens of thousands of English weavers found themselves with no work to do. A few days before the *Mayflower* reached America, King James reluctantly called his first Parliament in six years, prodded into action by those who wanted England to join the Thirty Years' War. Raising money for rearmament should have been its principal concern. By the time the House of Commons met in early 1621, the crisis in the economy had instead become the chief topic for debate.

As unemployment rose, members of Parliament frightened one another with talk of a peasant uprising. 'Looms are laid down', one wrote in his journal. 'Every loom maintains forty persons ...

the farmer is not able to pay his rent, not for want of cattle or corn or money. The fairs and markets stand still.' Most alarming was a sudden scarcity of money. For its bullion, the Royal Mint relied entirely on private citizens bringing in plate or old coins to be recast, but the inflow of silver ceased entirely. Not a single silver coin was struck at the mint between April 1619 and March 1620, and very little in the twelve months after that.

As British governments do, King James appointed a committee to investigate. It reported that things were very bad, and offered many explanations. It said something must be done, and then the king did nothing. A contemporary spoke of 'that great and generall dampe and deadnesse ... which we unhappily feele at this day.' In 1622, a year after returning from America, Jones died at the very bottom of the slump. He left a widow, sons and daughters, and an empty ship. Her ultimate fate is unknown, but most likely the *Mayflower* was scrapped in 1624.

Behind the slump lay many causes, but for the Pilgrims it was the consequences that mattered. In their early years in the New World, they could expect only fitful support from their backers and friends at home. In due course, seamen and merchants looked for ways to avoid another economic crisis of the same kind by widening their sphere of enterprise; and in doing so, maritime England turned its attention decisively across the Atlantic. But that did not occur until later in the decade. In the meantime, Bradford and his comrades mostly had to fend for themselves, or try to find allies on the western side of the ocean. And if they wanted help from heaven, they had to pray to a god of thunder, the terrifying deity of John Calvin.

6

AMERICA

Crossing Sinai

What man, if he be to goe a long and unknowne journey, will not hire a guide to conduct him? Or to undertake a voyage by water, to the East-Indies, Guiana or the Newfoundland, but desireth the most skillful pilot to goe with him? And shall not wee seeke unto God, and desire his direction from earth to heaven? From this old Aegypt to the new Ierusalem? If we doe not, we may well wander out of our way; and split the ship of our soules upon the rocke of condemnation.

–JOHN BARLOW, PURITAN TOWN
PREACHER OF PLYMOUTH, DEVON, IN
A FUNERAL SERMON OF 1618

More than a week had passed since the last full moon. The date was 9 November, 1620, and at last the *Mayflower* was nearing her journey's end on the coast of America. The men of the morning watch rang four bells to mark six o'clock, and turned the ship's hourglass on its head in almost complete darkness. Due west, a third of the way up the vault of the sky, the *Mayflower*'s helmsman would have seen a flickering orange point. It would be Arcturus, one of the brightest fixed stars with which an expert seaman could measure latitude. Below Arcturus and to its right in the north-western quadrant of the heavens gleamed the bulkier lamp of Venus.

Then, as dawn approached, a long, blurred horizontal shadow emerged from the gloom beneath the star and the planet. By seven, twenty minutes after sunrise, the shadow had hardened into a thick grey line. From the swaying deck, Jones and his crew made out a ridge of land, wooded with oak and cedar.

In cold but clear weather and at perhaps only ten miles, there would be no mistaking its identity. Robert Coppin, the second mate, had been there before. Eighteen years earlier another Englishman had described the headland's low sandy hills, its trees, and its shoals of cod, mackerel and bream, and given the Cape the name it has carried ever since. To seamen of Coppin's generation, Cape Cod's long sickle-shaped outline made a familiar landmark in the charts they could study before setting sail. It was, said an optimistic writer describing the voyage of 1602, a land 'faire and pleasant, resembling France, temperate and well-agreeing with our constitution'. For ships coasting for six hundred miles from Maine to Jamestown, the anchorage behind the Cape's northern tip had offered a safe haven for at least half a decade.

Landfall came as a relief after more than nine weeks at sea, but by itself it gave Jones no cause for satisfaction, and for William Bradford and his fellow Pilgrims the sight of Cape Cod brought with it new anxieties. Because of their false starts and foul weather – for many days, the winds were 'so feirce, and ye seas so high, as they could not beare a knote of saile,' Bradford later remembered – they were two months behind schedule. It seems that the *Mayflower* had found her way up the long slot of deep water that today forms the main shipping lane to Boston. Slanting northwestward on a naval chart, it passes between the dangers of the Nantucket shoals inshore and those of Georges Bank far out at sea. Even so, Jones had lost his way.

They were nearly 250 miles from the destination he had hoped to find, at the mouth of the Hudson River somewhere near the site of modern New York. And, within the belly of his ship, Jones's passengers were close to the limits of endurance.

Between the timbers of the *Mayflower* lay a wet, narrow space smelling of vinegar, vomit, stale meat, and overripe cheese. In daylight the lower deck resembled a long dim corridor. Partially blocked at intervals by nautical clutter, at night it was entirely dark. From deck to deck the headroom was no more than about five feet, or only four in places where the beams reached from side to side. A crouching man found his way impeded by a capstan for hoisting the *Mayflower*'s anchors, three masts, the bulkiest nearly two feet thick, and the dismantled hull of a shallop, or small boat. The rest of the crowded space was filled with human beings and their belongings.

After so long at sea, the indignities of the voyage threatened to reduce them to a demoralised rabble. 'A boisterous sea and stormy weather will make a man not bred on it so queasy sick,' wrote a maritime author of the day, Sir William Monson, 'that it bereaves him of legs, stomach and courage so much as to fight with his meate.' And yet everything we know about the *Mayflower*'s passage suggests that they strove to keep up appearances and to maintain decorum.

Even on the ocean, the English ranked each other in categories, carefully arranged in grades of wealth and social status. Twenty-four households travelled on the *Mayflower*. At least fifteen, with between them forty-nine members, were headed by an adult male who had lived in Leiden. The remaining nine households came from England; some apparently had Puritan leanings, of a less radical form, and it seems that some were purely economic migrants. We cannot be precise, because the passenger list does not refer to their religion, or their lack of it; it simply proceeds in order of deference. At the top were John and Katherine Carver, travelling with five servants and an adopted child. At the bottom of the list sat ten single men without families, land, or skilled occupations. Sadly, because Carver failed to survive more than a few months in the New World, we know little about him, beyond the fact that he was 'godly & well approved', as Bradford put it, and their first choice as the colony's governor. In the England of the period, a man of property naturally expected to serve as a local official.

It seems that the discipline he and Mr Jones enforced extended to hygiene. Next to scurvy, amoebic dysentery ranked as the worst marine affliction, the so-called bloody flux that had killed Sir Francis Drake. And yet in the *Mayflower*'s case, only one crew member and one passenger failed to complete the journey, the latter being William Butten, a boy of fifteen who died a few days before they sighted land. Perhaps, as some have argued, wine residues in the ship's planks helped prevent infection, since wine lees are mildly antiseptic. But this cannot have had more than a very marginal effect, if any at all. More likely, they held disease at bay by keeping their quarters clean, and always going up on deck to empty their bowels and bladders.

Whether or not they were hygienic, their presence created difficulties for Jones, since human beings occupied precious space. To fill out their earnings, seamen were given part of the hold for 'furthing', a stock of trading goods they carried on their own account for dealing freelance at either end of the voyage. On the *Mayflower*, the colonists and their stores would have limited the room available for goods of such a kind. Since seamen resented emigrants, animosity between them might provoke a mutiny: shipboard squabbles were commonplace at the time, mainly arising from low wages or from the failure to pay them at all. In 1605 an angry English crew had refused to take a cargo of colonists to Guyana. Instead, they mutinied and marooned them on the island of St Lucia, leaving them to starve or to be slaughtered by the Caribs.

Evidence of the unpleasant atmosphere on board the *Mayflower* survives in William Bradford's account of the voyage. He speaks of the ship's boatswain, who was 'a prowde yonge man, and would often curse, & scofe at ye passengers'. This comment takes on its full meaning when we bear in mind that the boatswain was the most senior member of the crew. Responsible for sails and rigging, he conveyed the master's orders to the sailors and took charge of the loading of the ship's cargo. Under his direction, passengers came on board and stowed their possessions. During the voyage they fell beneath his control. Since he had to be able to read and write – he had to keep a 'bosun's book' listing the ship's freight – his scoffing might be well-informed: from printed satires, or anti-Puritan jokes from the playhouse, he would know how best to needle a Separatist.

For all these reasons, Jones would be eager to disembark his passengers swiftly. So he decided to head southwards towards the Hudson. Within a few hours they came to a place where the glaciers that formed Nantucket Island and Cape Cod left on the seabed a shifting labyrinth of sandbanks and shoals.

A man with Jones's knowledge of England's coastal hazards would not try to find his way through them without a pilot. So, when they sighted the breakers, they swiftly turned back from a point somewhere close to a reef now known as Pollock Rip, where the modern chart shows as little as eight feet of water. Back they went northward by night for fifty miles, passing the buff-coloured ridge called the Highlands, close to the outer end of the Cape. At last the following day they rounded Race Point and entered the wide, shallow stillness of Provincetown Harbor, dotted then and now with a multitude of gulls, 'the greatest store of fowl that ever we saw'.

Behind the calm waters of the anchorage, William Bradford saw only savagery and terror. For him, it was a wild country already chilled by the first onset of winter, 'hedious & desolate', full of wild beasts and wild men. Four times on a single page of his manuscript he wrote the word 'wilderness' to describe Cape Cod. In front of them lay a desert, another word from his vocabulary: no inns, no habitations, but only woods and thickets.

He likened the Pilgrims to the apostle Paul, stranded by a storm on the island of Malta, but their predicaments seemed to be very different. Paul met inhabitants who warmed him by their fire, while the Pilgrims could expect only arrows from the native people. Behind them was the ocean, vast and furious, dividing them from what Bradford calls 'ye civill parts of the world'. Even so, he writes, they fell on their knees and gave thanks to God.

So Bradford remembered the occasion, when he described it in the early 1630s. His first narrative of the Pilgrim arrival had told a more positive story. It can be found in *Mourt's Relation*, a travel journal he co-authored with his fellow Pilgrim Edward Winslow, published in London in 1622. Intended for public consumption, to attract new investment and new settlers, it called the Outer Cape a 'goodly land', and it heaped praise upon the haven. Provincetown Harbor would safely hold a thousand ships, they said. It promised rich whale fishing, cod in season, and beyond the beach freshwater and timber for cooking fires.

Which version was correct? Was the Cape a goodly land or a wilderness? Neither account was objective fact of a simple kind, but in the space between the two narratives we find William Bradford himself. He lived a double or a treble life, as man of God, entrepreneur, and founder of a new commonwealth. In his account of the voyage, it was the Calvinist who held the upper hand, and because of that we can re-enter his imagination and experience the arrival as he would have done.

Bradford's Voyage

Somewhere out on the ocean, and amid the blast of a gale, one of John Carver's servants, John Howland by name, slipped off the wet timbers of the *Mayflower*. He may have been no more than twenty-one, a 'lustie younge man', says Bradford. Howland came up on deck and fell off, but before he hit the waves, he caught a rope that was trailing in the sea. It kept him afloat long enough for somebody to fish him out of the surging water with a boat hook within the short span of minutes before the cold froze his muscles and fatally weakened his grip.

Howland went on to spend five decades in America, acting as manager of a beaver trading post. Lusty young John became, in Bradford's words, a 'profitable member' of the community, not least when, much later, in a gunfight on the Kennebec River in Maine, Howland and his men killed an English fur-trading competitor. Howland lived on until 1673, surviving William Bradford by more than fifteen years. He and his wife, Elizabeth, founded a lineage with perhaps more descendants than any other *Mayflower* couple.

When he died, Howland left behind him his widow, ten children, and eighty-eight grandchildren, and an ample herd of cows, sheep and goats, but he also left something else. He owned an item that, like a key, unlocks the meaning of the journey as he and William Bradford understood it. The key is a Separatist book that Howland possessed, a commentary on the Bible written by a Hebrew scholar named Henry Ainsworth. In the book,

Ainsworth shows us how the Pilgrims used Bible stories and Calvinist theology to interpret the meaning of all their adventures.

We need the key because Bradford tells the story in such an unusual way. He describes the voyage and the arrival at Cape Cod in the ninth chapter of the first book of his history of New Plymouth, but in a manner that, if we are honest, most readers will find odd, or even evasive. The more often we read it, the stranger it becomes, like a message in code in search of decipherment.

Chapter 9 contains fewer than eighteen hundred words, and barely seven hundred concern the passage across the open sea. Another three hundred describe the landfall, the dangers of Pollock Rip, and the double back around Race Point. The remaining paragraphs consist of a long, eloquent contemplation of the wilderness, as Bradford first saw it. But in telling the story of the voyage, the Pilgrim left out almost every fact that most readers, then and now, would consider relevant or essential.

The name, design and dimensions of the ship and the number of crew members: none of these appear in Bradford's history, and he says very little about Jones. Historians have had to fill in the details from other sources, using a few clues that Bradford left scattered in his text. Chapter 9 leaves out the birth at sea of Oceanus Hopkins, son of a Pilgrim couple. It makes only the briefest mention of the death of William Butten. Bradford never talks about food, drink, armaments, pirates, the last view of land, or meetings with other craft, such as the Newfoundland ships, some of which he must have seen. He says nothing whatever about the route.

These gaps and omissions were unusual, even by the standards of his age. Travel books were popular, and navigation fascinated laypeople who had never set foot on a ship. When a later Puritan migrant, John Winthrop, kept his journal of his voyage to Massachusetts in 1630, he listed all the facts and figures that Bradford omits, and far more besides. Winthrop recorded sixteen calculations of the ship's latitude made, clouds permitting, with sightings of the noonday sun as the vessel, the *Arbella*, tacked westward from the Lizard along the forty-third parallel. He drew sketches of the coast of Maine and a rough map of the shore leading to the ship's destination at Salem. Winthrop even mentions the venison pies they ate when they arrived.

Bradford gives us none of this. From what must have been many incidents, during the sixty-six days between the English Channel and the Cape, he selected only very few, of which Howland's narrow escape was one. Before describing it,

Bradford tells us about another lusty youth, Howland's ungodly double, a 'proud ... & profane' seaman who jeered and cursed the seasick passengers, saying that he expected to dump half of them over the side before journey's end. It pleased God to smite the young man with disease, and he was tossed overboard himself.

William Bradford's most famous anecdote concerns a flaw in the ship. When the *Mayflower* left Plymouth, the wind was 'prosperous', says Bradford, for what he calls 'a season' – again, he does not say how long it was – until the ship encountered headwinds. Shaken and leaking, the ship struggled on against gales so fierce that the crew had to strike her sails and lie hull down among the steep waves, or risk losing her masts. During one of these episodes, as the *Mayflower* lay without a sheet of canvas to catch the wind, Howland came up on deck and was nearly lost. The flaw in the ship came to light when one of the beams that supported the main deck bent and began to crack.

Causing alarm and agitated discussion, the incident could not have happened at a worse moment. They were almost exactly halfway across. It would be hard to weigh the hazards of a return in winter past the Lizard against the risk of finding no means to make repairs in America. But, confident in his vessel, Jones eventually convinced passengers and crew that her timbers were sound underwater. As for the sagging beam, they heaved it back to the horizontal with an iron screw – these can still be seen today, in the few working windmills preserved in eastern England, used like a wheel jack to lift sacks of flour – and then the *Mayflower*'s carpenter wedged a post beneath it, supported by the lower deck.

And yet again Bradford leaves a hole in his narrative. The beam must have been more than twenty feet long and a foot in diameter. It would have been as heavy as six grown men. A joiner who knows English oak will tell you that such a beam will split only under extreme force from above. William Bradford never tells us how this could have happened, while the other beams remained unscathed. Perhaps the timber was rotten, which might explain why the splitting wood aroused so much anxiety. But Bradford never says that this was so, leaving rot merely as a possibility lingering in the margin. Even his account of Howland's narrow escape contains a perplexing feature. Bradford calls the rope that saved him a halyard, used to raise a topsail. Only a very shoddy boatswain would let a halyard dangle into the water, instead of making it fast to a cleat: Bradford offers no explanation.

But then why should he? William Bradford did not claim to be a seafarer. He did not write a sailor's yarn, dense with salty detail. For Bradford, the voyage possessed deeper meanings that mattered far more than blocks, tackle and belaying pins.

Bradford described a real voyage, experienced firsthand, but he carried his own heavy cargo of associations. In almost every sentence, he alludes to the Bible. Was Howland an ordinary young man? Or a junior Moses, saved from the water like the prophet when Pharaoh's daughter found him floating in the Nile? Were the crew of the *Mayflower* another grumbling batch of Jacobean sailors? Or, as they debated the cracked beam, did they act out the roles of the sailors who threw Jonah into the sea?

For Bradford, trained by reading commentaries on the Bible such as Henry Ainsworth's, each episode of the voyage carried a plethora of Christian meanings. In the splitting beam, he would see more than a damaged lump of wood. For him, it might represent the rot caused in the soul or in the Church, by sin or by strife. England was Egypt, the Atlantic was the Red Sea, and Cape Cod was Sinai. The stormy passage of the *Mayflower* re-enacted other voyages in the Bible: the ark of Noah, Paul's journey to Rome, and on the waters of Galilee the twelve disciples, with Christ as master of their fishing boat.

Inside the head of William Bradford, the Pilgrims mimed out these episodes of sacred history. When they reached dry land, they repeated another ancient formula. At Provincetown, the Pilgrims fell on their knees and thanked God, says Bradford. Again, behind his narrative lies a Hebrew model. It came by way of Bradford's knowledge of a Jewish ritual, the *birkat hagomel*, a ceremony of thanksgiving.

A First Thanksgiving

In 1618, the first prayer book for sailors appeared in print in England, written by a parish minister in the City of London. He had recently given a farewell sermon to the crew of the *Royal James*, bound for the Orient for the East India Company, and his book carried a dedication to its shareholders. Dr John Wood gave it the subtitle *Holy Meditations for Sea-Men*. It contained prayers to be read at sea, before a battle, during a storm, or at the funeral of a crewman.

Among the prayers he included one titled 'Thankes-Giving to God After Deliverance from a Tempest'. The clergy often read thanksgiving prayers, and under Elizabeth it became customary to draft new ones for every blessed occasion: the end of an epidemic, the Armada's defeat, or some bloody massacre inflicted on the Irish. Wood composed a seagoing version, using as raw material words and phrases from the Psalms to assemble a chorus in praise of the might and mercy of God. One psalm gave him more words than any other. This was Psalm 107, used later in the English rite for a burial at sea. It spoke of seamen engulfed by a storm who pray to God until he brings them to a peaceful harbour.

As a Separatist wary of official worship, Bradford did not care for prefabricated liturgy read from a book. However, the Pilgrims had all grown up with thanksgiving prayers, and every Christian had a duty to say such things. If the prayers followed the Bible, no one could object. So Bradford did the same. At the end of chapter 9, after his meditation on the American landscape, he also repeats verses from Psalm 107, words that describe the journey of Moses and the Israelites out of Egypt and across Sinai. 'When they wandered in ye deserte wildernes out of ye way, and found no citie to dwell in, both hungrie & thirstie, their sowle was overwhelmed in them,' writes Bradford, quoting the Psalm from the Geneva Bible, the translation used in early New England. 'Let them confess before ye Lord his loving kindnes, and his wonderfull works before ye sons of men.'

For the Pilgrims, these words carried a double meaning, arising from a Hebrew source. If Bradford turned to the notes Henry Ainsworth added to

Psalm 107, he would find Ainsworth quoting the medieval rabbi Maimonides. Writing about the Mishnah, the Jewish code of laws, the rabbi said that the words of the Psalm, including the verses quoted by Bradford, gave birth to the Jewish rite of thanksgiving. Maimonides listed four occasions when the *birkat hagomel* was compulsory: the healing of a sickness, the release of a prisoner, the end of a voyage, and the arrival of travellers at their destination. Ainsworth listed them too, and described the form taken by the Jewish prayer. It was a public confession of the goodness and majesty of God, of exactly the kind that the Pilgrims performed at Provincetown.

A year later, most likely in October 1621, after their first harvest, the colonists held the festivities commemorated by the modern Thanksgiving. Edward Winslow described them in two sentences. He mentions three days of feasting on game: wild-fowl shot by the English, and venison killed by the native warriors who joined the celebrations. This is more or less all he says, but Winslow's brief paragraph has given birth to a weary torrent of controversy. Did they eat turkey? Did they wear pointed hats? Was the event holy or secular, a wilder version of an English harvest festival? Did they call it a thanksgiving? Or was it something the native people termed a *nickommo*, a ritual feast or dance held to avert drought or sickness, to celebrate good fortune or bring victory in war?

Most likely, it meant one thing to one person and something else to another, as communal occasions always do. But if we could ask William Bradford to define the first Thanksgiving in America, he would point to something else. He would say that it took place at the instant of arrival, at the moment on Cape Cod when the Pilgrims fell on their knees to say the Jewish prayer. And yet even this act of devotion contained an undercurrent of melancholy, of a kind often found between the lines of Bradford's text. He likened the Pilgrims on the Cape to Moses, as the prophet gazed out across the plain of Jericho. At the end of the book of Deuteronomy, from a mountaintop Moses saw the promised land. As Bradford knew well, the prophet had crossed Sinai, but he never entered Canaan. Moses died, leaving his bones in an unmarked grave on the edge of the wilderness. In America an identical fate awaited half the *Mayflower*'s passengers and crew.

7

THE PLYMOUTH COLONY BEGINS

Comfort and Refreshing

> Though this had been a day & night of much
> trouble and danger unto them; yet God gave
> them a morninge of comfort & refreshing (as
> usually he doth to his children) … on munday
> they sounded the harbor, and founde it fit for
> shipping; and marched into the land.

> —WILLIAM BRADFORD, DESCRIBING THE FIRST
> ARRIVAL AT NEW PLYMOUTH

Almost the first thing they saw at Provincetown
on 11 November was a school of whales. Every
day they played around the *Mayflower* as she lay at
anchor, like the little fleets of dolphins she must
have passed ten weeks before along the coast of
Devon. There were so many that Jones compared
Cape Cod Bay to the whaling grounds of the
Arctic. 'If we had instruments and means to take

them, we might have made a very rich return,' the
Pilgrims later wrote, but for the time being the
whales were spared. Harpoons and nets were among
the items they had failed to bring. When they tried
to shoot one of the creatures from the deck, the
gun exploded into pieces in its owner's hand.

A century later, in the 1740s, a local shipowner,
Benjamin Bangs, kept a remarkable journal of his
own, an account of the bay as the Pilgrims would
have known it. Bangs described the great schools
of blackfish, the Cape Cod name for pilot whales.
At the time of year when the *Mayflower* arrived,
Bangs often saw them fill the waters between
Provincetown and the shore five miles away at
Truro, each one as much as twenty feet long.
When the wind changed to come from the northwest, it left them stranded in immense numbers
along the beach. On a single day in late October
1747, the people of Truro killed six hundred of
the creatures. As far south as the modern town of
Wellfleet, incidents of slaughter on an even vaster
scale continued until as late as 1912, when in the
age of petroleum the pilot whale at last began to
lose its value as a source of oil for lighting or for
lubrication.

The blackfish might stand as a symbol of the
strange new world that the Pilgrims entered. It
was an altered and vastly magnified version of

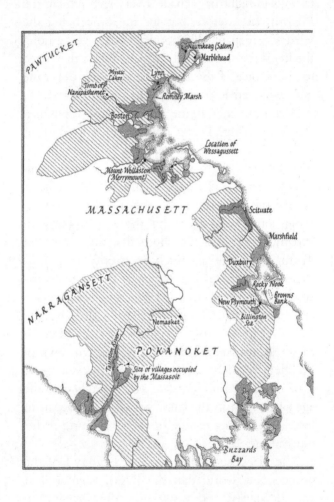

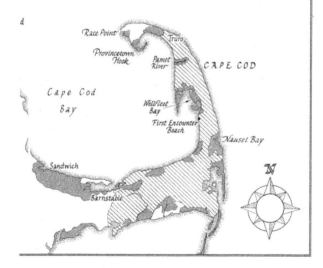

Southeastern New England, 1616–40

Areas of salt marsh (approximate)

Approximate extent of areas occupied by native people before the epidemics of 1616–19

Names of principal groups of native people are marked in capitals

0   5   10   15   20

Miles

ATLANTIC

OCEAN

d

Race Point

Provincetown Hook

Truro

Pamet River

CAPE COD

Cape Cod Bay

Wellfleet Bay

First Encounter Beach

Nauset Bay

Sandwich

N

Barnstable

what they knew in the old. Pilot whales belong to the same marine family as the dolphins of the English Channel, but here in America these creatures existed in numbers unimagined, just as the falls and the sweep of the rivers of North America far surpass the valley of the Trent. Reading the works of Captain John Smith had prepared the Pilgrims up to a point, but previous English seafarers like Smith had mostly come to this part of the Atlantic coast much earlier in the year. They had never described the blackfish, and never travelled far inland.

In the pilot whales, the Pilgrims saw what Smith told them they would find: an abundant store of value in nature, holding out the promise or the temptation of riches. For the first time, they also realised how unprepared they were, how few tools they had, and how long it would be before anything better than survival could be achieved. A long process of education lay in wait. It was going to be a matter of trial and error, mistakes and successes, improvising and adapting. They took old skills and English models and either made them fit the New World or discarded them if they did not.

Captain Smith made one dangerous omission. He had neither endured nor put into words a northeastern American winter, and while the Pilgrims must have known something about the climate, they had little with which to compare it. Although the Thames sometimes froze, it was a rare event, like the great frost at Christmas in 1607, chronicled in detail precisely because it was unusual. It was not a customary feature, like the ice that blocks rivers in New England between January and March. Cold of a very un-English severity was the second thing the Pilgrims noticed on Cape Cod, straight after the whales.

It began when they had to wade ashore at Provincetown – the earliest detailed chart shows that water deep enough to float a ship began only half a mile from the beach, and even a small boat had to stop a long way out – and then it became steadily more acute. By the first week of December, more than six inches of snow covered the land. In a small boat men found that damp clothing froze on their backs like iron, and coughs and catarrh evolved into fatal illness.

In his account of their first winter in America, Bradford only mentions scurvy by name as a cause of death among the colonists. However, he also refers to the filthy condition of the sick. At sea, for whatever reason, they had escaped the mariner's scourge of amoebic dysentery, but Bradford's comments suggest that the disease struck them with its full force after their arrival in New England. If scurvy was the principal agent of mortality, then the dreadful fact is that it could have been avoided. By 1620, ships' surgeons in the East India service were already well aware that lemon or lime juice prevented the disease, although it took another century or more before the Royal Navy began to carry fruit rations on every long voyage. Dysentery was quite another matter: apart from trying to keep themselves clean, and drinking water to ease the dehydration caused by diarrhoea, the Pilgrims could do nothing about it.

By the time the spring returned, forty-four of the passengers had died, and nearly half the crew. The first four to succumb, including Dorothy Bradford, William's wife, had died before the Pilgrims first saw New Plymouth. The fate of Dorothy Bradford – she fell into the sea and drowned – remains mysterious, but the other three were those we might expect to perish soonest. They were either old or very young. The first was Edward Thomson, a servant, probably in his teens, who died on 4 December, but the next was seven-year-old Jasper More, and then James Chilton, on 8 December: in his mid-sixties, Chilton was perhaps the oldest man on the *Mayflower*.

And yet, as disease began to take its toll, the Pilgrims also made journeys of discovery. These expeditions finally took them to Plymouth Bay, on 10 December, and led to their choice of a place to settle. There are two ways to tell the story of what occurred. We can simply follow the familiar sequence of episodes, narrated many times by many writers, as they explored Cape Cod on foot, and then with the shallop, and fought their first fight against the native people at First Encounter Beach near Wellfleet. Or, alternatively, the opening weeks can be seen as a series of meetings with objects or creatures like the black-fish, phenomena that, like the number of pilot whales, defied an English imagination.

Ranging and Searching

First, the outline of events. To sustain a colony, the Pilgrims needed timber, game, fresh running water, a flat expanse of earth for corn, shoals of fish, and a harbour – and, if they could find them, a wide river leading inland, and native people willing to sell beaver skins. Some of these elements existed on the Cape, but the full combination most certainly did not. South along the shore, the mouth of the Pamet River was visible from Prov-incetown, but after a few miles it led to a dead end. It was tidal and salty, and around it the ground was dry. That was the damning flaw of the place: rain simply vanishes into the sandy soil. Province-town has little water of its own, and although

Truro has aquifers, they lie deep beneath the surface.

Added to that, the terrain was exhausting. An outwash of gravel and sand from melting glaciers created the Outer Cape, and to the south it formed a wide, dense belt of low hills in their dozens with no obvious route through them. It was unattractive as a place to settle. Even in 1790, Provincetown had fewer than five hundred inhabitants. At the end of the eighteenth century the entirety of Cape Cod all the way to Sandwich had little more than seventeen thousand, so that much of the land still lay empty.

The first expedition was simply a landing, fifteen or sixteen armed men going ashore on 11 November to reconnoitre the land around the harbour. The second was more ambitious, and began on 15 November. Again it involved only sixteen men, but over three days they saw their first native people in the distance, found signs of graves and cultivation, and reached the Pamet. Most famously, they discovered a buried cache of corn and a ship's copper kettle. They filled the kettle with corn and carried it back to the *Mayflower* slung on a pole between two men to serve as seed the following season. They intended to pay for it, and indeed they did so eventually, but not before the incident caused their first clash with the natives.

The shallop remained unfit for use until 27 November, but then a third expedition was possible, more than thirty strong. The boat followed the men as they marched along the shore. Again they found corn, and more graves, but also their first native encampment, two houses made from bent saplings covered with mats. They were uninhabited, but filled with bowls, trays, dishes, pots, and an English basket. When they returned to the ship on 30 November, they began to debate what they had seen: the time for urgent discussion had arrived, because as the weather grew worse, further missions by sea would become impossible. Supplies were running low, disease began to appear, and the *Mayflower* could not be relied on to linger on the coast. If they were to leave Provincetown and find a new place to settle, they would have to do so very swiftly.

They decided to make a last journey of discovery, by sea around the inside of the Cape. Most of all, they wanted to reach an estuary, which the second mate of the *Mayflower* believed he had seen on an earlier voyage. Led by John Carver and by Miles Standish, a former soldier who had sailed on the *Mayflower* as the Pilgrims' military advisor, but also including Bradford, Howland and Edward Winslow, the party set out on 6 December. They did not find the estuary – none of any size existed nearby – and they lost their mast and were nearly wrecked in a gale at the entrance to Plymouth Bay. But they did find the site of New Plymouth, where at last they landed on 11 December. The *Mayflower* followed on 16 December, the Pilgrims began to come ashore, on or near Plymouth Rock, and so the colony began.

New Plymouth did not have an estuary, but it was the best place they could find. Dense woodland lay behind it, and the site had flowing water – as always, Bradford singles out for comment 'the running brooks' – and it had an adequate harbour, ringed by sandbanks but accessible with practice. Inland they found cornfields left by the native people, most of whom had died in the epidemics. It was also defensible, thanks to some high ground they called Burial Hill.

Several hundred yards inland, the hill rose above the cornfields and might serve as a redoubt. This must have seemed all the more necessary, because during their exploration of Cape Cod the Pilgrims had suffered the consequences of their theft of corn. As they broke camp at dawn on the sands, a party of thirty or forty native people had attacked them with a hail of arrows. Led by Standish, the party had to fight them off with their muskets.

Such was the bare schedule of the journeys that the Pilgrims made, but their engagement with the Cape took another form as well. There was a narrative, a plot that unfolded as the Pilgrims looked for a suitable site to settle, but they also encountered a succession of new and bewildering images and objects. Of these, by far the most disturbing was a Native American grave that they found on Cape Cod on 30 November somewhere in the flatland along the Pamet valley. In a narrative written by Edward Winslow, it was described with a precision highly unusual at the time. This was a sign of how odd the Pilgrims felt it to be.

Seeing traces of a recent burial, they began to dig. They found first a mat, then a bow, and then another mat. Beneath it was a board more than two feet long, painted and carved, with incisions or slots at one end that made it resemble a crown. Between the mat they found layers of household goods: bowls, dishes and trays. Underneath them was another mat, which covered two bundles. The larger one contained a sheet of canvas, a cassock of a kind worn by sailors, and a pair of breeches. Inside them were the skull and almost entirely decomposed body of a man.

To their astonishment, the skull had strands of yellow hair. Around the body there were European goods: a knife, a pack needle for securing baggage, and pieces of iron. Dark red powder, with a strong smell, covered the remains. They found the same powder in the second, smaller bundle, encasing the bones and the head of a small child. Strings and bracelets of white beads enveloped its limbs, and beside the remains was another small bow. The Pilgrims took some of the finest articles and filled in the grave.

Archaeology did not yet exist in England, even in rudimentary form. Nearly forty years passed before a doctor from Norwich, Sir Thomas Browne, published in 1658 the first account of prehistoric and Roman remains ploughed up by English farmers. Not until the 1680s did a museum curator in Oxford begin to write reports about stone tools found in the earth. And yet Edward Winslow took notes of painstaking accuracy, giving details that can be exactly verified from later excavations. The twin burial at Pamet closely resembles a similar interment found in Massachusetts at Marblehead, near Salem, in 1874. The excavators discovered the same powder and beads, a similar mixture of native and European goods, and the same manner of placing a child beside an adult.

Perhaps the dead at Marblehead and at Pamet were victims of the epidemics that had swept the coast: the Pilgrims saw many graves, suggesting that some appalling catastrophe had befallen the inhabitants. And yet Winslow displays not so much horror as fascination, as well he might. No contrast could have been greater with the burial practices of his homeland. By 1620, the churchyard of an English parish remained the resting place of the vast majority – the wealthy had taken over the chancel, inside the church and at the front – but it had become an unholy space, used for keeping geese or pigs or grazing cows. Few grave markers of any kind existed: only very rarely does one find a gravestone set up before 1660. If the churchyard dated back to the time of the Norman Conquest, by now it might contain thousands of skeletons, with no record of their resting place. Every plot had many occupants.

After the English Civil War, attitudes began to change, but in the gravedigger's scene in *Hamlet*, Shakespeare portrayed Jacobean cemeteries as they were, muddy and unkempt, with their scattered bones and skulls and shallow, reused graves. Inside the church, another regime existed for the wealthy, and in the four decades before the *Mayflower* there was a rush to build carved monuments, with the painted effigies that still survive on so many tombs. Even so, it was the effigy that mattered, and the inscription. The physical remains of the deceased were an irrelevance.

For Calvinists, this was entirely logical. For them, death was final and absolute, an instantaneous divide, the point at which the soul passed entirely beyond the reach of human beings, either to damnation or to eternal life. It might make sense to erect a carved monument as a commemoration of rank, or to flatter the living members of the family, but caring for the corpse served no purpose. In the graves he found on Cape Cod, Edward Winslow encountered people for whom exactly the opposite was true, for whom the dead might be ever present. For them the ornamentation of the cadaver was a duty. The native Americans left precious trading goods with the remains as a mark of respect for the departed.

Within the next three years, Winslow's readiness to pay close attention to the customs and the language of the native people whom he met came to be an essential asset of the Plymouth Colony. It was critical for their survival. Equally fundamental was another early event: the signing of the Mayflower Compact, that document sometimes seen as the origin of American democracy.

The Mayflower Compact

If the first creatures they saw at Provincetown were the pilot whales, the first thing they did was to sign the Compact, before the first men landed, before the women went ashore to wash clothes, and before the carpenter began to reassemble the shallop. Like the blackfish, the Compact was a mingling of the familiar and the very new. The Pilgrims took English models, and then radically transformed them to fit new conditions.

Forty-one adult males put their names to the document on 11 November, because Carver and his colleagues wished to put a stop to argument and grumbling in the ranks, dissent that might give rise to mutiny. The problem arose because the *Mayflower* had strayed north beyond the domain of the Virginia Company, entering territory where the patent for the colony had no legal force. Because of this, says Bradford, some of the 'strangers' on the ship – meaning men who had not come from Leiden, but joined the party in England – pointed out that they could not be compelled to obey orders.

So, to maintain unity and discipline, they drafted and signed the compact. When the Pilgrim narrative *Mourt's Relation* appeared in London in 1622, it included the text, but the authors Winslow and Bradford added a preamble that puts the situation very clearly: 'it was thought good there should be an association and agreement, that we should combine together in one body, and to submit to such government and governors as we should by common consent agree to make and choose.' As we shall see in a moment, the words the writers chose were loaded with significance.

The Compact was what an English lawyer would call an enabling document. It was not a constitution as such. The Pilgrims drew up a combination or a covenant, creating 'a civill bodie politick', and they gave it the powers to make 'just & equall lawes, ordinances, Acts, constitutions & offices' for the general good of the colony. But they did not say exactly what those rules would be. For this reason, and because it was clearly improvised, it has become commonplace for historians to play down the importance of the document, as though it did not have a fundamental role to play.

It is also fashionable to claim that writers and politicians in the northern United States invented a Pilgrim myth in the nineteenth century. It is said that this Yankee myth gave the *Mayflower* and New Plymouth far more significance than they deserved, compared with Jamestown, or with the Great Migration of Puritans to Boston in the 1630s. Some argue that the Mayflower Compact was no more than a short-term, temporary measure, drawn up in a hurry, containing nothing new and nothing original. That being so, the argument runs, it could not possibly be the foundation stone of American democracy, but was simply one source among many.

We can debate the legacy of the Compact as it was seen by later generations, or we can ask how a Jacobean Englishman or Englishwoman might have regarded it. Did *they* think it was merely a temporary fix? Or was it much more? Would the Mayflower Compact have struck *them* as something new and different? If it did, and if it contained some radical elements, going beyond the usual English way of running a town or village, then the case for the Compact is proven. If it was new, it was new. If it possessed originality, then it deserves to be given back its status as the earliest manifesto for a distinctive, American form of democratic government.

What did the document mean to William Bradford? It was certainly improvised, but in his eyes there was nothing mythical or temporary about it. For him, the Compact always remained fundamental, a permanent, necessary source of authority as long as the colony lasted. If it had simply been a short-term fix, the Compact would have ceased to matter in 1630, when the Plymouth Colony obtained a definitive new patent from the Earl of Warwick, as president of the Council for New England. Instead, Bradford and Winslow made it plain that the Compact remained very much alive.

In 1636, they codified the rules of the Plymouth Colony in a new Book of Laws. On page one, they called the Mayflower Compact 'a solemne & binding combinacon', and they treated the Compact and the Warwick Patent as the double-barrelled source of the colony's right to exist and to run its own affairs. If one or the other could claim seniority, then it was the Compact, not the patent. This was because the Compact depended on the vote of the governed, while Warwick issued his patent under authority delegated from King Charles.

In the same Book of Laws, they added an extra paragraph that explains how they interpreted the documents. They say that they came to America as 'freeborne subjects of the state of England'. Helpfully they explained the meaning of the words. Freedom meant that nobody could force on the colony any 'imposicon law or ordnance' – and, incidentally, an imposition meant a tax – except 'by consent according to the free liberties of the state & Kingdome of Engl. & no otherwise'. In other words, obedience to the law required freely given consent, just as it did in the paper they signed at Provincetown.

In a crisis, if the Pilgrims could not agree to a law passed in England, and if they had to choose between obedience and liberty, then the king would have to be discarded. In the Book of Laws, they wrote out the form of words used when every new freeman of the colony swore allegiance to it. All the men pledged 'to advance the growth & good of the severall plantations', but they also swore to be 'truly loyall to our Sovereign Lord King Charles'. Some time later, doubtless during the English Civil War, they neatly crossed out the mention of the king. Although the Mayflower Compact began with a promise of loyalty to the monarch, in extremity he could be deleted from the constitution, while the consent of the governed could not. The people outranked the Crown.

All of this happened a very long time after the landing at Cape Cod. It might be thought that the question of resistance to the Crown never arose at the moment when the Compact was signed. Actually, it *did* arise, or almost certainly so, in the mind of the *Mayflower* Pilgrim William Brewster. Because of his education and his earlier career, Brewster the old Scrooby postmaster stands out as the man most likely to have drafted the document. He owned works by an author notorious for justifying rebellion in circumstances where the sovereign failed to honour his side of his bargain with his subjects.

In 1622, the Archbishop of Canterbury ordered the public burning of books written by a German Calvinist called David Pareus, professor of theology at Heidelberg. They were, said the archbishop, 'seditious, scandalous and contrary to the scriptures', but four volumes by Pareus sat on Brewster's library shelves at New Plymouth. Among them was the most seditious of them all, the professor's commentary on Saint Paul's letter to the Romans. No book within the Bible carried more weight with the Pilgrims than this one, and David Pareus gave it a startling new interpretation.

In a famous passage, Saint Paul told Christians to obey their rulers, the powers that be, because they were divinely ordained. Boldly, Pareus reread this to mean that the same Christians had a *duty* to overthrow a tyrant, and especially an irreligious one, because such a man was clearly an enemy of God. 'Obedience hath certaine limits,' Pareus wrote. 'When tyrants go about to force their subjects to manifest idolatry, or to some wickednesse, against the expresse word of God; in this case the scripture commands us, that in no wayes we obey such tyrannical Edicts, but that every man, according to the condition of his calling, make resistance.' Of course, Brewster did not insert anything of such an outspoken kind in the Mayflower Compact. All the same, if this was the world of ideas within which he lived, then we would expect to find them leaving radical traces within the words he did employ. And so we do, though mingled and blended with other language that was more common.

At Provincetown, they had to find a substitute for the patent granted by the Virginia Company. So whoever drafted the compact modelled it partly on the words these patents usually contained. Examples survive, from 1619 and 1622, when the company gave planters the power 'to frame and make orders ordinances and constitucions'. Although the original patent granted to the Pilgrims has been lost, it would have included a similar clause. Whoever drafted the compact simply carried over the same language. This was because the need for it arose only from an accident of seafaring, and not from defects in the original document.

Any educated Jacobean would have noticed something else as well. When the Pilgrims used the term 'a civill bodie politick', and awarded themselves the power to make laws and ordinances, they used phrases from the royal charters that gave English boroughs their rights and powers. Early in the reign of King James, many towns renewed their charters, tightening up the wording to prevent legal challenge by people who, for example, disliked paying local tolls or taxes. They included towns that Brewster and Christopher Jones knew intimately: Doncaster, Harwich, and Retford in Nottinghamshire. All three obtained new charters between 1604 and 1607. If New Plymouth was a sort of colonial borough packaged up and shipped across the Atlantic, then again it made sense to use the same sort of language.

So was the Compact trite and commonplace, a ready-made replica of the arrangements by which any town in England already ran its affairs? No, most definitely not. A mass of legalese, designed to thwart any hostile litigation, an English borough charter often ran to four thousand words, twenty times longer than the compact. It was intended to be exclusive. Most of the new charters placed the right to rule in the hands of a few citizens, like the maritime oligarchy to which Jones belonged at Harwich. That was not the case at Provincetown. Brief, clear, more a statement of principles than a charter, the Compact carried the signatures of the vast majority of the men on board, and it treated them all equally. Menservants did not sign, and because dates of birth are missing for many passengers, we cannot be certain exactly how many adult males made the crossing. But at the very least the forty-one signatures accounted for 90 per cent of the men on the *Mayflower*.

During the reign of Elizabeth, experiments in democracy took place in small English towns and villages, but in this respect, the number of those who signed the Mayflower Compact went far beyond them. A case in point was Blyth in Nottinghamshire, three miles from Scrooby. Like the Plymouth Colony, Blyth had a common house, a common store of arms, and an annual election. Every April the townspeople gathered to choose a mayor, and they recorded the outcome in a town book that still survives. In 1587, the lord of the manor of Blyth died without an adult male heir, and the people of Blyth seized their chance to assert themselves.

They rewrote the language used for an election to make it clear that the townspeople could freely elect whomsoever they wished, without following a recommendation from the local landowner. Again, the words they used closely resembled those of the compact. At Blyth, the citizens decided that in future the mayor would be 'chossen by the consent of all the inhabitants … he will endeavoure himself to doe the best that he cane for the common wealthe of the towne'. They widened the franchise, from eleven voters in the 1570s to as many as ninety-two in the 1590s. Even so, the electorate represented less than one-third of the adult males at Blyth, so that 'all the inhabitants' meant something far less than it did at New Plymouth.

Although it drew on experiments like the one at Blyth, the compact went much further, simply by allowing every freeman full participation. As for its guiding principles, they flowed from another, deeper source in the political ideas that Brewster came across either at Cambridge or during his period as an aide to William Davison in the 1580s. Brewster certainly owned a copy of a manual of government written by Sir Thomas Smith, a royal official. In the 1560s and 1570s writers such as Smith began to speak of England as though the realm were really a republic, like the ancient city of Rome. Of course they had a queen, but she ruled by way of consent, expressed through Parliament and the Privy Council – or so they suggested. According to Smith, in a sentence evoked at Provincetown in the language of the Compact: 'A common wealth is called a society or common doing of a multitude of free men collected together and united by common accord and covenauntes among themselves, for the conservation of themselves aswell in peace as in warre.'

When the Pilgrims picked the term 'association' to describe the document they signed, again they chose a word with a loaded meaning embedded in the politics of the Elizabethans. Only in the 1580s did people start to use the word in this sense, to mean a paper signed by a number of people with a common purpose. This usage of the word became current in the name of the so-called Bond of Association drawn up by the Privy Council in 1584. Drafted by Lord Burghley and Sir Francis Walsingham, it circulated up and down the country, attracting the signatures of thousands of local dignitaries and members of the gentry. They swore to resist by force of arms anybody who made an attempt on the life of Queen Elizabeth, or tried to claim the throne.

In the 1980s, the British historian Patrick Collinson showed that the Bond of Association was itself a republican document. It was drawn up in such a way that, if Elizabeth died without an heir, the signatories of the bond would elect a new Protestant sovereign. Brewster entered public service, working for one of Walsingham's closest aides, during the period when the bond was very much a talking point.

Were all these echoes of earlier documents merely unconscious or coincidental? Perhaps they were: but given what we know about William Brewster, it seems unlikely. Assuming that he drafted it, he assembled the Mayflower Compact from a mosaic of the best precedents he could find. He made it simple and clear, but he also filled it with resonance. He did not insist on a religious creed, or require sectarian faith from those who signed it. In 1620, a Roman Catholic could have put his name to it without offending the pope, since all the compact demanded was a brief, ecumenical nod in the direction of King James. It contained not a single phrase with a specifically Puritan meaning or source.*

The Pilgrims drew up the agreement in a new location, at the moment of creation of a new colony. They did so in terms that, two decades later, could be used as a rationale for outright resistance to the Crown. This, the right of disobedience, existed within the language of the Mayflower Compact from the very start. Most radically of all, they produced a document that nearly every man signed, including those who in England were only laborers. This was all very new indeed, as new and different as a school of pilot whales.

The Meeting with Samoset

As the winter went on, hardship and deaths continued. After the *Mayflower* arrived at New Plymouth, five weeks passed before the first Sunday when the Separatists could gather for a Sabbath

---

* The Mayflower Compact uses the word 'covenant' to refer to the agreement between the colonists. Although the word could have religious connotations, equally often it simply meant a legally binding contract.

assembly on land. Until that point, the colonists remained mainly on the ship, where so many of them had died: six in December and another eight in January. In the meantime, they had laid out a settlement with two streets and plots of land around them. On Christmas Day, they began to build a common house to hold stores and provide temporary shelter. They also started to make an emplacement for cannon on the hill.

Thanks to atrocious weather and the toll taken by sickness, each of these tasks took far longer than it should: the common house remained unfinished until 20 January. At times as few as six or seven men and women remained on their feet. As the number of deaths neared its peak, they began to see signs of more activity among the native people of the interior. Up to that point, they had caught glimpses of fires in the distance, but now, on 16 February, a man out shooting wildfowl saw a band of twelve warriors. He took cover, then hurried back to the colony to sound the alarm. In the next few days the Pilgrims made ready to receive an attack. To fortify the colony, Jones and his seamen unloaded four pieces of artillery from the ship and dragged them up Burial Hill.

The onslaught never came, but death from disease continued. They were still dying in March, thirteen that month, even as the weather began to brighten. Edward Winslow's wife, Elizabeth, died on 24 March, the last day of the old year 1620, as the English reckoned their calendar at the time. On 3 March they heard birdsong, and on 7 March they planted their first vegetables. On the same day Governor Carver led their first fishing and hunting expedition to a lake named Billington Sea and to other ponds close by. Within weeks he would be dead, apparently from a heart attack while working in the fields in April. Less than two months later his widow, Katherine, died too.

Bradford never said much about John Carver. Only one seventeenth-century historian gives us even the briefest character sketch, and that was William Hubbard, author of an official history of New England, begun in 1682. However, Hubbard clearly had sources that have since been lost, and so his comments about Carver carry weight. Hubbard writes about his piety, his humility, and his public spirit, but also he refers to the man's 'public purse'. Carver, he wrote, 'disbursed the greatest part of that considerable estate God had given him for the carrying on of the interest of the company'. Carver also lived long enough to accomplish the principal duty of any colonial governor: diplomatic affairs, the making of pacts and treaties. Shortly before he died, he reached an accord with Massasoit, the foremost sachem (or chieftain) of the native people of southeastern New England. It came about by way of the intervention of two intermediaries.

On Friday, 16 March, 'a fair warm day', as they completed their fortifications at last the settlers saw a man break cover close to their huts. He was tall, with long black hair swept back from a shaved forehead, beardless, and almost naked, except for a leather loincloth. He carried a bow and two arrows, one tipped with a warhead and the other not: that was symbolism. This was a man the English mariners on the coast of Maine called 'Somerset'. It was no doubt a garbled, joking sailor's version of whatever his name was in his own language.

Three years later, far away near Boothbay Harbor in Maine, an English naval officer met Somerset, or Samoset, as Winslow knew him. The officer, Captain Christopher Levett, remembered Samoset as a sachem himself. He was a leader among his people, eager to talk and trade beaver pelts, and to make an alliance with Levett against their enemies, the raiding Micmac people from farther up the coast. Captain Levett recommended him as a man 'very faithfull to the English'. Samoset, Levett said, had 'saved the lives of many of our Nation, some from starving, others from killing'.

Samoset also spoke English, learned from the seamen at Monhegan Island. Already, English and

French were becoming the trading dialects of the coast, as the economies of western Europe began to annex the region. The native languages of the inhabitants are generically known as Algonquian, but this is actually a family of different languages, and as Levett pointed out, two native people from settlements separated by as little as seventy miles could understand each other no better than the English could the Welsh. Today, the Native American linguists who keep alive the ancient tongues of Rhode Island or Massachusetts do not claim to know the languages of Maine or Quebec. As Levett remarked, 'They were glad to use broken English to express their mind each to other.'

So it was with Samoset. He strode up to the Plymouth colonists, and he began to pour out a description of the coast, its people, its chiefs, and their military resources. By now, he clearly knew that these details fascinated the English, just as they enthralled Ferdinando Gorges at old Plymouth fifteen years before. Samoset asked for beer, and so the Pilgrims gave him brandy: doubtless they and the sailors had long since finished off the *Mayflower's* ale. That afternoon Samoset began to explain the politics of the hinterland, and the reasons why the native people had seemed so likely to attack.

He told the Pilgrims that bitter recollections remained, arising from the activities of Thomas

Hunt, an earlier visitor. Hunt was a ship's master who came with Captain John Smith on his voyage to New England in 1614. By the time the Pilgrims came ashore, Hunt himself was dead. He was lost at sea or succumbed to disease in 1619, after a trading voyage or two to Russia: his will survives, and so does a record of the bullion Hunt carried to Archangel. In his lifetime he almost destroyed New England before it began.

Thomas Hunt was a religious man who made bequests to pay for Good Friday sermons by 'a godlie preacher' in his hometown.* However, in Cape Cod Bay, at the site of New Plymouth and farther east and around towards Hyannis, under cover of commerce Thomas Hunt tricked onto his ship some twenty-seven people. Twenty came from Patuxet, the native name for Plymouth, and seven from among the Nauset, who lived along the Cape. Hunt took them captive and carried them back across the Atlantic, to be sold as slaves in Málaga: as Captain John Smith put it, Hunt 'sold those silly Salvages for Rials of Eight'.

Stories of the incident spread around the region, and worse was to follow. Another English skipper massacred a trading party of native people with a barrage of shot from his 'murderers', small

---

* Aldeburgh, in Suffolk.

shipboard guns carried for use at point-blank range. Because of episodes such as this, in 1620 another ship's captain sent out by Gorges, Thomas Dermer, very nearly met his end at the hands of the inhabitants of Martha's Vineyard. Not long before the arrival of the *Mayflower*, he lost all his crew and had to flee south to Jamestown.

It was not surprising, then, that the Plymouth colonists encountered hatred and distrust. However, among the captives taken by Hunt was another native, a man about to join Samoset in helping them bargain with Massasoit. This was Tisquantum, the Native American who became famous as Squanto, the friend of the Pilgrims. At Málaga, Spanish monks saved him and his fellow prisoners from slavery, and Tisquantum found his way to London. There he learned English before he shipped back to America with Dermer. Thanks to what he saw by the Thames, he stood ready to mediate between the Pilgrims and the native people inland.

In the meantime, in the same city of London, Thomas Weston faced a gathering crisis of a different kind. As the depression deepened in 1621, men like him found their business affairs disintegrating. They turned to dangerous expedients, including some that took them outside the law.

8

THE SECOND ACT

The Mystic and the Thames

> You may guesse in what case we are (for all our
> fair shewes) when neither Lord Maior, Alderman,
> farmers no nor whole companies, as the East
> Indian ... are able to hold out and pay their debts.
>
> —THE NEWSLETTER WRITER JOHN CHAMBERLAIN
> TO SIR DUDLEY CARLETON,
> 10 NOVEMBER, 1621

Very early one morning, in the darkness between
one and two, a barge filled with heavy sacks
approached a wharf beside the river Thames. The
sacks weighed ten tons, and if any had split or burst,
they would have spilled a fine white powder onto
the mud or the timbers of the jetty. A group of
men waited for the barge at a spot on the north
bank almost opposite the Globe Theatre. Their leader
was one Philemon Powell, aged about twenty-five.

There was, it seems, some delay, an altercation by the water's edge. At last a deal was struck, and Powell and his accomplices loaded the sacks into carts or wheelbarrows. They trundled them along the lane that sloped up and away from the river towards the sheds and houses of Bread Street Ward, where that night they made their delivery.

On the wharf with Powell was Andrew Weston, younger brother of Thomas. Both men were under surveillance. An informer patrolled the wharf, Brook's Wharf, between Stew Lane and Queenhithe, a few hundred yards upstream from London Bridge. He spotted Powell and the sacks, which contained alum, more scientifically known as aluminium sulfate. It was a chemical essential for the textile trade, because it helped to fix dyes into woollen cloth.

Smuggling alum was a racket, one of many in Jacobean England, a contraband activity that could yield a profit of nine pounds per ton, before paying off those whom you had to pay off. This, it seems, was one of the ways in which Thomas Weston tried to recoup the losses he made from the voyage of the *Mayflower*. The legal records describing the incident give it no precise date, but others that survive show that Weston was dealing heavily in alum in the spring of 1621. He had every reason to turn to desperate alternatives, because the expedition to New England had been a commercial fiasco.

As the settlers emerged from their first winter, in London their backers soon learned that the venture had fallen at its first hurdle. The *Mayflower* made a swift return passage, leaving America on 5 April and docking back in England on 6 May, but she came back empty, with neither fish nor fur. That was the worst possible outcome for Weston and his associates. One mishap they could cope with, but only one: the error in navigation, which had caused Jones to disembark his passengers a long way from the intended destination by the Hudson.

The investor group quickly dealt with that. They obtained a new patent for the colony from the Council for New England. The council happily granted the permission required for the Pilgrims to occupy a spot north of the fortieth parallel: the document, the so-called Peirce Patent, hangs today in Pilgrim Hall at Plymouth, Massachusetts. This, however, was just a legal matter, necessary but not sufficient. It did not pay their bills. As the economy shrank, the investors found their resources diminishing too. Instead of writing off the Pilgrims instantly, they began to assemble finance for a second voyage, to reinforce the colony. Even so, it took another two months to prepare the second ship, the *Fortune*, and she was small.

She had a volume of only fifty-five tons. Although she carried thirty-five new settlers, she was almost entirely devoid of supplies and trading goods. The *Fortune* did not reach New England until November. When she did so, at first she hovered oddly around Cape Cod, causing alarm: reports from the native people suggested that she was a hostile French vessel. William Bradford armed his men, loaded the cannon on Burial Hill, and prepared to blow the Frenchman out of the water.

At last the *Fortune* entered Plymouth Bay, and she was passed as friendly. Her passengers swiftly panicked after seeing the conditions at the colony and after listening to the customary words of encouragement from the *Fortune*'s crew, seamen as jaundiced as those on board the *Mayflower*. They very nearly re-embarked and left, until the *Fortune*'s master talked them out of it, promising in an emergency to carry them on down the coast to Virginia. Even so, as Bradford recorded, 'ther was not so much as Bisket, cake, or any other victials, neither had they any beding, but some sory things ... nor over many cloaths.' But at least they added labour. Almost all the passengers were grown men but young, and they had their uses: one of them was Philip De La Noye, the distant ancestor of Franklin Delano Roosevelt.

In London, the economic depression worsened. Since England had no banks, there were no banks to fail, but there were many loans to foreclose and many speculators on the brink of ruin. Within the *Mayflower* investor group, the stronger men clung on, and staked their hopes on the *Fortune*, but Thomas Weston had reached the end of the road. He spiralled down towards insolvency. Worse still, he offended the authorities, by way of 'wilful contempt and abuse offered to the State', as they put it when later they issued a warrant for his arrest.

Was Thomas Weston a rogue? Perhaps, but if he was he had good company. That year, many men saw their businesses go under, and it should not be surprising that commercial ethics went the same way as their money. In the same month that the *Fortune* reached New Plymouth, the Lord Mayor of London fled his creditors, emptying his house and vanishing one dark night. As for the alum scam, it was commonplace: in 1620, the Crown prosecuted more than a hundred merchants, up and down the length of the kingdom, for illegally shipping in four thousand tons of the stuff. The fraud, if that is what it was, arose because of the way in which the Crown had riddled the economy with perverse regulations and monopolies, creating incentives for cheating.

A racket as lucrative as this could not be expected to last. Unhappily for Weston, in April 1621 the king gave a new patent to a man called Guest, making him an official searcher for alum. Guest would receive a reward for each ton of contraband he found. A copy of the patent survives, in the immaculate archives of the Lord Treasurer of the time, Lionel Cranfield, along with a set of documents that relate to Weston. The informer at Brook's Wharf contacted Guest, it appears, and Guest filed a lawsuit against Weston in June in the Court of the Exchequer, the forum that handled matters relating to royal revenues. Guest demanded unpaid customs duties on the smuggled alum, and tried to impound the consignment. Predictably, Weston had bought it on credit: if he lost the case he faced ruin.

For merchants such as he, reliant on IOUs, the only working capital available was reputation. Once that was gone, they were virtually doomed. Of course, the Exchequer jury found against him, and so Thomas Weston's affairs began to unravel. For one thing, the two men who bought the alum from Powell were throwing all the blame in his direction, insisting that Weston alone was liable for the heavy penalty imposed by the court. It came to no less than £345, a huge multiple of the profit that Weston had hoped to make. The sum was far beyond his reach.

Weston survived for a little while, since he had a few weak cards left to play, and a last flimsy line of credit, but the inevitable could not be delayed for long. As we shall see, Weston reached his lowest ebb in the early months of 1622. At the same time the Plymouth Colony very nearly collapsed, and for reasons that were closely related. In the meantime, before the *Fortune* arrived, Bradford and his comrades had begun to lay some foundations for the future.

Samoset and Tisquantum

When the Pilgrims met Samoset in March 1621, they gained access to the networks of trade between the native people, the French and the English that circled back and forth along the shores of the Gulf of Maine. This was not a new phenomenon. At least as early as the 1590s, sachems from among the Micmac people to the east and north had begun to act as middlemen, translators, and procurers of beaver pelts. However, there was something very unusual about Tisquantum. It swiftly emerged after Samoset introduced him to the Pilgrims on 22 March. It transformed a fraught and dangerous situation.

In the six days since he first came striding out of the forest, Samoset had been entirely friendly, but on this part of the coast his value was limited. He was not a local man. With him, on 18 March, he had brought five warriors: tall long-haired men like him, but dressed differently, with deerskins wrapped around their shoulders and long leggings that Winslow likened to the trousers worn by the Gaelic Irish. They offered the Pilgrims a few skins, but these exchanges remained hesitant on the English side, with Carver and his men still nervous about the danger of an attack. At one point, two or three warriors appeared a few hundred yards away on the top of Watson's Hill, making threatening gestures, until Standish took out a patrol and warned them off with his muskets. A better intermediary was needed.

Tisquantum arrived with Samoset, bringing a few skins to trade and some fresh dried red herring – Winslow carefully noted details such as these – and, as we saw, he too spoke English. In his case, however, he had learned it in a remarkable location, while staying at the London home of John Slany, a merchant who ranked far above the likes of Weston in the commercial hierarchy.

Slany lived on Cornhill, at the very centre of the City. Since 1610, he had been treasurer of the Newfoundland Company, a small colony, even smaller than New Plymouth. It was so small that the annual supply ship from England carried among its stores only twenty-four gallons of beer.

Slany owed his stature not to this disappointing venture but to his position among the Merchant Taylors, the largest of the London livery companies. We do not know the exact dates of Tisquantum's period in London, but it seems to have been in 1617. In that year Slany, aged about fifty, served as one of the company's three wardens, while in 1619 the Merchant Taylors chose him as their master, a post carrying so much prestige that the Dutch ambassador attended his election.

A man of substance, John Slany had close ties to the largest clients of Christopher Jones: in 1619, Jones's associate William Speight joined the ruling committee of the same company, and John Slany's brother Humphrey imported wine on the *Mayflower* less than nine months before she sailed to America. We can also be sure of something else: that if the social life of the City of London bore any resemblance to the same thing today, then Tisquantum would have swiftly become a celebrity, in the street, in taverns, or paraded at formal dinners.

Was it simply a coincidence that Tisquantum turned up again at New Plymouth in the spring of 1621, just as the Pilgrims emerged from their first winter? Perhaps: but it seems equally likely that ships which arrived off Maine or Virginia in March knew about the *Mayflower*, that news about her travelled up and down the coast, and that Tisquantum came looking for the Pilgrims when he heard the word 'London'. At this point, Jones and his command were still anchored in Plymouth Bay. As soon as Jones and Carver heard the name 'Slany' from Tisquantum, they would have known that they had found someone they could trust.

Tisquantum spoke the language of the Wampanoag, the people led by Massasoit. He could describe in detail the city from which Jones had sailed, with its merchants, its ships, its king, its wine, and its weapons of war. He could also explain that while most Englishmen might be vicious hypocrites like Thomas Hunt, an occasional exception could be found. At the Newfoundland Company, Slany gave specific instructions that native people should be treated with respect.

However Tisquantum came to be there at exactly the right moment, he made the essential introduction to Massasoit. That same afternoon of 22 March, with sixty of his warriors the sachem himself appeared above the settlement. Actors in a pioneering drama, playing parts in a scene to be repeated many times in the ensuing history of the British Empire, from the Ganges and Lucknow to the African veld, the Pilgrims made peace on behalf of the Crown of England.

They had no Maxim guns or Enfield rifles, but they did have Standish, his muskets, and the ordnance unloaded from the *Mayflower.* They also had a small stock of trading goods, knives, bracelets, a copper chain for Massasoit, and alcohol too: Winslow mentions the brandy they gave the sachem to drink. And, of course, they had Tisquantum as translator.

In the name of King James, Edward Winslow crossed the Town Brook towards Massasoit and then opened the negotiations, offering trade, a peace treaty, and an alliance against his enemies. This Massasoit required, because of the dangers he faced from his enemies to the west, the Narragansett of Rhode Island. Hostages were exchanged as sureties, with Winslow remaining on the perilous side of the water. Then Massasoit forded the stream, under an armed escort led by Standish, and walked up the short but steep slope towards the English houses.

His conference with John Carver took place in a half-finished dwelling in the colony, where the Pilgrims had placed a green rug and some cushions. Again, it was a scene awaiting re-enactment many times in a later period. To the beat of a drum, Governor Carver kissed the hand of Massasoit. As the sachem returned the compliment, they sat down on the cushions and the rug, and Massasoit ate and drank the food and liquor he was offered.

According to the Pilgrims the deal they struck contained six heads of agreement: essentially, a pact of non-aggression, and an alliance against enemies who might attack either the English settlers or Massasoit and the Wampanoag. We have to say 'according to', because no record exists from the side of Massasoit to show how he understood the terms of the arrangement. At this early stage the language barrier had not yet entirely disappeared. Tisquantum lacked a perfect command of English. And although in London some people had studied the languages of the Algonquians, the vocabulary they knew came from Virginia, where the idioms and diction were entirely different.

For the short term, the agreement reached on 22 March evidently marked a turning point, since the military threat from Massasoit fell away. That is as much as we can honestly say. The peace held: but how and why did it do so? Even Bradford, describing it more than two decades later, offered no explanation. The reality, perhaps, was that the English at New Plymouth had accepted a territorial boundary, whether they understood it or not. So long as they remained within a small perimeter around New Plymouth, separated from the native people's territory by a cordon of swamps and dense forest, Massasoit would leave them in peace.

The Fate of the Fortune

After the commercial failure of the *Mayflower's* voyage, William Bradford and his fellow Pilgrims knew that it was imperative to get a cargo of fur and timber back to London as soon as possible. They swiftly turned the *Fortune* around and sent her home with pelts acquired to the north along the Mystic River and from Massasoit. One of the Separatists named Robert Cushman sailed back with her on 13 December, 1621, taking two hogs-heads of beaver skins, otter skins, clapboard, and sassafras, worth about four hundred pounds. Then, five weeks later, disaster struck her too, when on 19 January she met a French warship off the coast of the Vendée, to the north of La Rochelle.

Cushman and the *Fortune* were unlucky, but the circumstances were typical of the period. Navigation remained imperfect, and naval affairs were always liable to disrupt or divert the path of western enterprise. The French skipper caught them not far from the fortified Île d'Yeu, but this lies more than 350 sea miles from Land's End and the Lizard Peninsula. It seems that the *Fortune* had made a familiar error. She mistook the long snout of Brittany for the southwestern end of England, and then she strayed off down the French Atlantic coast at the worst possible time.

Under the law of the sea, even though England and France were at peace a French captain could legally seize the *Fortune* if she was a pirate, or in reprisal for plunder taken by English ships, or if she was aiding France's enemies. Only two months previously, as part of their defiance of King Louis XIII, the Huguenots of La Rochelle had sent out their *armée navale* to fight the royal fleet, and given it a thrashing. The king's ships fled back into harbour, while the Huguenots prowled up and down the coast. The fortress on the Île d'Yeu remained in the hands of the Crown, but any English vessel coming close was liable to search and seizure in case she was ferrying supplies to the rebels. The French warship stopped and boarded the *Fortune* and carried her back to the island.

It soon emerged that she was neither a pirate nor carrying contraband. All the same, the French governor seized her guns, cargo and rigging. He locked her master in a dungeon and kept Cushman and her crew under guard on board the vessel. He also confiscated the manuscript of *Mourt's Relation*. After thirteen days, he let them go, with the book but minus the beaver skins. They made it back into the Thames on 17 February, 1622.

They found commerce in London paralysed by the depression and the *Mayflower* investors in deep trouble, and none more deeply so than Thomas Weston.

By this time he was already nearly ruined, and the loss of the *Fortune*'s beaver fur dealt the final blow. When the alum racket blew up in his face the previous summer, Weston wrote one IOU after another as he tried to carry on trading, but he had very nearly reached his limit. For many years, he had expected the Pilgrims' friend Edward Pickering to guarantee his debts, but by the time the *Mayflower* reached America, their ties were already weakening. Each man came to distrust the other. In March 1621, Pickering came over to London from Amsterdam to try to settle their differences, and an agreement was patched together; but as his problems mounted, Weston continued to issue IOUs which he expected Pickering to honour. By early 1622, the relationship had collapsed entirely, after a heated argument in London. Weston killed it for good by having Pickering arrested for debt, and at about the same time he broke with the rest of the *Mayflower* investors. He sold his share in the venture for whatever they would give him. By this time, Weston was being pursued in the courts for payment for a consignment of Welsh woollen cloth, and he owed still more money to the men who had bought his smuggled alum and to the Crown. The authorities were determined to recover Weston's unpaid fines and customs duties.

Few men attempted anything as daring or as dangerous as his next manoeuvre. As the *Fortune* docked in London, Thomes Weston made one bold last gamble. The records of what happened remain in Cranfield's papers, as crisp and legible now as they were four hundred years ago.

Weston had fitted out another ship, the *Charity*, to sail from Portsmouth with a cargo of settlers and artillery, accompanied by a smaller fishing vessel called the *Swan*. He obtained an export license from the Privy Council to send the cannon to New England. Issued on 17 February, 1622, the day on which the *Fortune* reached the Thames, the license covered thirty pieces of ordnance. They included big guns each weighing nearly two tons. Allegedly intended for the use of the Plymouth Colony, the consignment came from the royal arsenal at the Tower of London, but it never reached America. It appears that Thomas Weston planned to run the guns elsewhere and then sell them to the highest bidder. There would be many takers in the North Atlantic, Arab pirates, Huguenots, Dutchmen or Spaniards, all of them in need of extra armaments.

News of the imminent departure of the *Charity* came to the attention of the men who ran the alum monopoly. They reminded the Lord Treasurer about Weston's debts to them and to the king. Weston had vanished from his London home, and from what Mrs Weston told them on the doorstep, it seemed that he was preparing to flee to New England. Lionel Cranfield swiftly alerted the authorities in Portsmouth, and they found Philemon Powell, posing as the purser of the ship. With him were eighty colonists, bound for New Plymouth and Massachusetts Bay.

Under arrest, Powell refused to talk. Because this was a very serious matter, Cranfield sent an Exchequer judge down to Portsmouth to interrogate the suspect. Unimpressed, Powell kept his mouth shut, claiming that by law no servant could be made to give evidence against his master. On 21 March, the exasperated judge reported back to Whitehall. Three days later Lord Cranfield ordered Powell's detention in the Fleet Prison in London.

Thomas Weston, meanwhile, had managed to evade arrest, hiding behind the silence of his accomplice. He had the gall to petition Lord Cranfield for Powell's release, arguing that he was losing five pounds for each day that the *Charity* lingered in Portsmouth Harbor. Then Weston disappeared entirely, only to surface briefly in New Plymouth the following year, after crossing the Atlantic disguised as a blacksmith. Most likely, he travelled on a Devon fishing vessel, and then he quietly slipped off one or another ship at one of the fishing posts along the coast of Maine.

Meanwhile, in the spring of 1622, the rest of the *Mayflower* investor group were wondering what to do next. Some were close friends of Pickering, who wanted to file suit against Weston: that autumn Pickering did so, issuing a futile subpoena. His case had little prospect of success, seeking money that Weston did not have, and tortuous litigation in London could not save New Plymouth. Whatever the long-term outlook, the colony urgently needed supplies that year. The investors did the best they could.

Led by two of the original *Mayflower* investors, James Sherley and John Pocock, at first they struggled. They could barely assemble enough money to pay for twenty tons of stores and send thirty passengers across the ocean. So in the spring Robert Cushman approached John Peirce, the London merchant who had obtained the new patent from the Council for New England. Peirce agreed to help finance another voyage, and somehow he and the *Mayflower* investors raised four hundred pounds. This was still a modest sum, but at least it was enough to buy thirty tons of supplies and trading goods and a ship called the *Paragon*.

Even so, she did not leave London until 1 October, and the voyage ended almost as soon as it had begun. The ship had barely reached the English Channel when she sprang a leak in a gale. Two weeks later she was back in the Thames. Her second attempt fared little better, and nearly ended in catastrophe. In January 1623, the *Paragon* set off again, with 109 passengers, many of them women and children. By the middle of February, she was only halfway across the Atlantic when she came close to sinking in another storm. At the storm's height, to save the ship, the master cut away the mainmast. With three men at the helm, the *Paragon* struggled back to Portsmouth, but minus her superstructure, shorn away by the sea.

Hearing of her return, Pocock and Sherley promptly told Peirce to repair the vessel and send her out again within fourteen days. When he did not, they went to court and sued him. Their attempt to rescue the colony ended in yet another exchange of recriminations. Four years later Peirce was still demanding compensation in the courts. An extra reason for the animosity lay in the fact that Peirce had apparently tried to double-cross both his fellow investors and the Pilgrims.

Six months before the *Paragon* sailed out on her first voyage, Peirce had gone to the Council for New England and asked them to amend the patent in such a way as to make himself and his business partners the landlords of the Plymouth Colony. It seems unlikely that this was outright swindling; probably Peirce simply wanted a sort of insurance policy, an element of collateral for the money he put up to finance the ship and her stores. When the Pilgrims, Sherley, and Pocock complained, the authorities upheld the original patent. Even so, the dispute rumbled on until John Peirce died.

The *Paragon* affair had been a shambles, but during the course of 1622 the Pilgrims had achieved something else, less tangible but with far-reaching effects of its own. Quite apart from founding a new colony, they had also helped to invent journalism in its modern form.

Two Greyhounds and the **Weekely Newes**

When the *Fortune* reached London stripped of her cargo, she still had on board the manuscript of *Mourt's Relation*. The Pilgrims had an excellent chance of finding a publisher, partly because Edward Winslow had trained as a printer in London and knew the book trade, but also because

Mourt's Relation was a fine piece of work. Fresh, exciting, and narrated in the clearest English, it told with a mass of visual colour and the odd joke or two the story of the colony's first year. The book began in England, on the way out of Plymouth Sound, and it ended in America after the first Thanksgiving. It went on sale in London, at a shop in Cornhill only yards from the home of John Slany, at the very time when a new vogue for topicality created a ready market for this sort of thing.

London had fewer than twenty printers, but the city had ten times as many booksellers. Under King James their business grew almost as fast as sales of wine and silk. In 1620, more than 400 new books hit the streets to satisfy a rapidly expanding reading public. Edward Winslow had served his time as an apprentice under a printer named John Beale, and in his search for new titles Beale tried pretty much everything.

Beale published not only travel writers, but also self-help books (*Directions for a Maide to Choose Her Mate*, of 1619), as well as sermons, sheet music, ballads, histories, how-to books on arithmetic and handwriting, and cautionary tales of city life. Another Beale title was something called *The Roaring Gallantes, Contayning a Short Narracion of the Lifes and Deaths of William Nicholls and John*

Welsh, Broker: sadly, no copy seems to survive. However, perhaps the boldest of London's book entrepreneurs were two men called Bourne and Butter. They became the founders of the English newspaper.

Edward Winslow certainly knew Nicholas Bourne, because at his bookshop Bourne stocked the titles that Beale had printed. Everyone in the business knew Nathaniel Butter, because he was the most audacious and flamboyant bookseller of his time. Butter began to publish sensational news as far back as 1605, when he issued a gruesome account of a murder in Yorkshire, with a sequel describing the execution of the culprit. In 1608, after publishing the first edition of *King Lear*, he followed it up with *Newes from Lough-Foyle in Ireland*. It chronicled the equally bloody career of O'Doherty, an Irish rebel from Donegal.

Books such as these were one-offs, not periodicals, but then in 1618 serial publications known as the first *corantos* went on sale in Amsterdam to meet the demand for regular news about the war breaking out in Germany. As the *Mayflower* lay at anchor off Provincetown, the earliest English translations of these *corantos* appeared in London. The following autumn, the first true English newspaper was born, when on 24 September, 1621, someone called 'NB' published the first issue of a weekly. It was called the *Corante* and subtitled *Weekely Newes,* but it apparently survived for only seven editions. Most likely, 'NB' was either Bourne or Butter, sheltering behind initials in case of official disapproval.

Then, in May 1622, as the Pilgrim manuscript sat in a printing shop awaiting the typesetter, a second wave of periodicals began to appear. Soon afterwards, Butter and Bourne joined forces to dominate the new market. On 15 October, they began to publish a weekly newspaper called *The Relation.* It ran without a break until the summer of 1624, when the first editor died during an epidemic. Filled with news of foreign wars, natural disasters, and the doings of kings and queens, it firmly established a taste for topical sensation, available to anyone who could afford twopence to buy a copy. Butter and Bourne had their own connections with the Pilgrims; and in London they did more than anyone else to create the environment in which the Plymouth manuscript found readers.

Of course, the two men lived in close proximity to the *Mayflower* investors: that came about simply because London was so densely concentrated. Nathaniel Butter lived in Bread Street Ward, where he attended the same church as the *Mayflower* investor John Pocock. The newspaper office was

Butter's shop, at the sign of the Pied Bull on Watling Street, a few yards from Pocock's front door. It was Bourne, however, who supplied a direct link with the Pilgrims, an affiliation they could not do without.

For nine years, Nicholas Bourne had an apprentice called John Bellamy, a young man with radical views. Many years later, when he was Colonel John Bellamy, part of the Puritan leadership in London during the civil war, it was revealed that in his youth Bellamy belonged to the group of semi-Separatists who met across the river in Southwark. These were the very same people who acted on behalf of the Pilgrims in the year of the comet, in their early negotiations with the Virginia Company.

John Bellamy clearly knew Edward Winslow, and like his employer he knew a commercial opportunity when he saw one. Early in 1620, Bellamy finished his time as an apprentice, but he went on working with Bourne until, at some time in 1622, he set up his own shop a few yards away, at the sign of the Two Greyhounds in Cornhill. There he began to publish and sell books. Among the very first was the Pilgrim narrative. Close behind it came Bellamy editions of the works of William Bradford's beloved author, the Hebrew scholar Henry Ainsworth, volumes bound and printed with such skill that they remain a pleasure to examine today, on paper with barely a mark of age.

At the end of June, as the second wave of newspapers started to go on sale, John Bellamy obtained his official license to print the story of the Plymouth Colony's adventures. It bore a title intended to appeal to exactly the same appetite for vivid news of current affairs.

Although historians call it *Mourt's Relation*, when it first appeared on bookstalls it carried a much longer title. Cascading down the page in such a way as to attract even the most jaded browser, it ran for eight paragraphs, filled with the names of Indian chiefs. Of course it began as though it were a *coranto*: the book, said the title page, was *A Relation or Iournall of the Beginning and Proceedings of the English Plantation Setled at Plimoth*. Two years later, they came up with a simpler title for Winslow's second book of Pilgrim adventures, but it was directed at the same audience. John Bellamy published that book too, and it was called *Good Newes from New-England*.

For the next twenty-five years, Bellamy went on issuing books relating to North America. He did so far more consistently than any other London publisher and printer. No method exists for quantifying the impact they had, but we can be sure of one thing. Colonies did not survive by themselves. They needed supplies, reinforcements, and new flows of stores and capital, and so they needed publicity too. Without the Pilgrim books published by John Bellamy, this would have been lacking. Since Bellamy learned his trade from Bourne and Butter, we can say with confidence that Puritan America relied on journalism from the very start: almost as much as it depended on the beaver, on Tisquantum, and on Massasoit.

9

A NEW WORLD

Diabolical Affections

Three things are the overthrow and bane, as I may term it, of Plantations ... 1. The vain expectation of present profit ... 2. Ambition in their governors and commanders, seeking only to make themselves great ... 3. The carelessness of those that send over supplies of men unto them, not caring how they be qualified: so that ofttimes they are rather the image of men endued with bestial, yea diabolical affections, than the image of God, endued with reason, understanding and holiness.

—Edward Winslow, 1624

The Pilgrim fort on Burial Hill looked east across the sea and west towards the forest. As late as 1830, an official map showed that even then the light and shade of the woodlands behind New Plymouth reached to within a thousand yards of the water's edge. In the time of William Bradford the cleared margin between the beach and the trees was far narrower still. One August day in 1623, a sentry posted on the parapet of the fort would have seen emerging from among the oaks and pines a procession of men and one woman. All of them were naked from the waist up.

They numbered as many as 120, and they were painted, some black and some yellow, but mostly a purple-red, the colour of mulberries. Their dark uncut hair was greased with oil. On their shoulders or behind them they carried or dragged as gifts the carcasses of slain deer and a turkey. At their head, most likely, was Massasoit, with his long knife slung across his muscular chest on a cord. The black skin of a wolf would have encircled his shoulders, while behind his neck there hung a pouch of tobacco.

As he descended the wooded slope towards the Pilgrim town, and followed a path that led along the north side of Burial Hill, Massasoit would have looked up and seen on a pike above the fort a severed human head, a few months old. In the summer sky close to it a scrap of linen flapped or dangled in place of a flag. The linen too was coloured red, but red of a different shade, the dull red of dried blood.

What Massasoit made of the severed head we cannot say, but the intention of the Pilgrims was clear. On 14 August, Massasoit, his warriors, his fellow sachems, and one of his five wives joined in celebrating the second wedding of William Bradford. The governor made sure that the head and the blood-soaked rag were starkly visible above the fort, as reminders to Massasoit that the Pilgrims were men of terror as well as men of God. For this period, the most detailed source is Edward Winslow's *Good Newes from New-England*, and its opening paragraph praises the work of divine providence for 'possessing the hearts of the salvages with astonishment and fear of us'. But anxiety and alarm were not one-sided, and the English felt them too.

Writing for public consumption, Winslow manfully defended the colony's achievements, and especially those that concerned security. Profits remained elusive, but the Pilgrims were 'safely seated, housed and fortified, by which means a great step is made unto gain', he wrote. As we shall see, much of *Good Newes* is military history, an account of the exploits of Miles Standish as he quelled an attempted assault on the Pilgrims by the people of the Massachusetts. It was the head of a Massachusetts warrior that Standish and Bradford stuck up on a pole, and his blood that dyed the linen. But interwoven with this chronicle of violence were other themes that preoccupied

Winslow and William Bradford alike. In the second
period of the colony's history, the fear of conspiracy
or civil strife became for them an overriding
concern.

During the first eighteen months in America,
the secret of survival was morale. In the next phase,
this remained the case, but the relevance of morale
expanded to encompass more than physical endurance. It widened to include the need to prevent
the colony from falling victim not to external
forces, but to its own internal discontents, or worst
of all to a combination of the two. This was the
motive for Bradford's brutal gesture of erecting a
decapitated head on a spike. It was something far
from customary in the England of the time, where
felons were hanged but beheading was reserved
for the most dangerous of offenders, English traitors or Irish rebels. It was a gesture of deterrence,
aimed perhaps at some of the colonists as well as
at Massasoit.

In the long second act of the drama at New
Plymouth, the central episode was a deadly fracas
at a place called Wessagussett, at the southern end
of what is now Boston Harbor. At Wessagussett a
ragged band of new settlers sent over from England
by Thomas Weston established a little colony of
their own; and when it collapsed into indiscipline
and chaos, the outcome in the spring of 1623 was

a bloody clash with the native people. As we shall see, this was how the head of a warrior came to be mounted on Burial Hill.

For William Bradford and his comrades, the affair at Wessagussett would serve as a grim reminder that the success of their community was still far from guaranteed. And the most dangerous threat to their survival might lie within themselves, if they succumbed to the human frailties that destroyed Wessagussett. Edward Winslow feared that the Plymouth colonists might still fall victim to what he called 'diabolical affections'. By that he meant the inner agencies of sin and degradation which, according to Calvinist theology, always lay in wait within the human soul to subvert the work of godliness.

Disorderly Wessagussett

Phase two of the Plymouth Colony had begun in the winter of 1621–22, a few months after the departure of the *Fortune*, and in ominous fashion. The Narragansett people of Rhode Island made apparent threats of war, sending over a sheaf of arrows wrapped in the skin of a rattlesnake: Bradford sent it straight back, stuffed with bullets. Doubts also arose about Tisquantum when he fabricated a story that Massasoit was planning his own attack, apparently as a means to restore his own status as a necessary mediator. This enraged Massasoit. Under the terms of his pact with the Pilgrims, he had every right to demand that Tisquantum be handed over to him for punishment.

This Bradford refused to do, but he could not afford any further disagreements with Massasoit at a time when the colony remained insecure. As yet, Bradford had no idea of the fate that had befallen the *Fortune*, but he knew how little the Pilgrims possessed by way of resources. In order to survive, and to live at peace with Massasoit and the other people of the region, the colony needed supplies and trading goods from home and new settlers who were able-bodied and self-sufficient. In fact, during that year and in 1623 the colony suffered a drain on what small reserves it had, and one that very nearly brought it to its knees. For this, they could thank Thomas Weston.

By now Weston was a ruined man and a fugitive. Even so, with financial help from John Beauchamp, another of the original *Mayflower* investors, he managed to send across the Atlantic another small craft, the *Sparrow*. She made landfall in Maine, joining the rest of the modest English fishing fleet in those waters. Somehow, too, Weston saved Philemon Powell from prison and secured the release of the *Charity* from arrest at Portsmouth, along with now only fifty or sixty passengers.

With the *Swan*, the *Charity* duly set sail and reached New Plymouth in midsummer, but when she arrived the thirty guns were missing. Their fate remains a mystery, but Weston's foes were quick to allege that the worst possible crime had been committed. Weston's brother Andrew sold the cannon 'for extraordynary and excessive gaine to the Turkish pyrates or other enemyes or strangers', the Pilgrim investor James Sherley claimed in legal papers. The guns were certainly sold to someone, but no proof exists that the buyers were pirates. Gunrunning to corsairs was an offense that would have sent the Weston brothers to the gallows, but no serious attempt was made by the Crown to pursue them. The authorities knew that the cannon had not reached New England; but they cared far more about the money the Westons owed in unpaid fines and taxes.

Before he went to ground, leaving his wife to cope with years of litigation, Weston wrote a final letter to Bradford, dated 10 April, 1622. Carried on the *Charity* or the *Swan*, and arriving nearly three months later in New England, it consists of excuses, diatribes against his enemies, and empty pledges of help. Weston also candidly admitted that the latest reinforcements he had sent to

America were not England's finest. 'Now I will not deney that ther are many of our men rude fellows, as these people terme them,' he wrote. 'Yet I presume they wil be governed, by shuch as is set over them; and I hope not only to be able to reclaime them from yt profanenes that may scandalies the vioage, but by degrees to draw them to god.'

Wary as ever, Bradford did not believe it. For him Weston's letter marked his final loss of confidence in his former backer. When Weston turned up at New Plymouth, in disguise, he cadged some beaver skins and supplies before heading to Virginia. Perhaps Weston had done his best, but he created for the Pilgrims more problems than he solved. On the *Charity* and the *Swan*, he sent over raw new settlers with inadequate supplies, and in doing so, he put the colony in grave danger. The native inhabitants of southern New England could not afford to allow into their land parasites who upset the economy they had created.

If the Pilgrims added something to the life of the region, by way of trading goods, or by assisting the native people against enemies inland or up the coast, then they might serve a purpose. If, on the other hand, the English became a leech on the area's resources, consuming other people's corn and game and offering little in return, then they had no legitimate reason to be there and should be expelled.

Weston's new settlers failed this test at a time when the Plymouth Colony could least afford to make mistakes. Within a few months of the arrival of the newcomers, the Pilgrims reaped their second harvest of corn from the little fields laid out around New Plymouth, but it was meagre. Crop raising in England and America alike required intense labour, by way of weeding and the application of manure, and in the New World without carts and livestock everything had to be carried and done by hand. But during the growing season of 1622, again the Pilgrims found their attention diverted from cultivation to defense.

An English ship fishing on the coast brought news from Virginia of a native uprising, which came close to destroying the settlement at Jamestown. Bradford promptly ordered the construction of a blockhouse on the top of Burial Hill, with emplacements for six cannon. The effort required took precious time away from agriculture. Since they were mostly too poorly nourished for manual work, the effect was all the worse, leaving food reserves depleted. Bradford also blames Weston's new settlers for stealing corncobs as they hung on their stalks in the fields, but the facts of the case are disputed.

There is an alternative version of what took place more sympathetic to Weston's men, and written by a different type of migrant. The author was an English lawyer and adventurer, Thomas Morton. He arrived in New England at some point in the middle of the 1620s and made himself the leader of a small fur-trading settlement at Mount Wollaston, between New Plymouth and Boston. In due course he quarrelled violently with the Pilgrims.

Since the middle of the nineteenth century, historians have argued about Morton, his reliability, and the true explanation for the mutual hatred between him and William Bradford. Since Morton was a man who enjoyed drink, dancing, and making fun of Puritans, and since he may have been another Roman Catholic, it is hardly surprising that his account of events fails to match the story as told by a Separatist. Nonetheless, Morton must be treated with respect. Published in London in 1637, but apparently written much earlier, his book *New English Canaan* contains details that can only have been learned by somebody who knew the landscape intimately, and had listened carefully to the native people around the shores of Boston Harbor. He differs fundamentally from Bradford.

Morton agreed that Weston's men were wasters – 'many of them lazy persons', he writes – but he accuses the Pilgrims of pushing them out of New Plymouth, because they might topple the Separatists from their position of control. According to Morton, Weston always intended that the beaver fur trade should be the basis of the colony, and the men he sent were entirely suitable for that purpose. The Pilgrims, Morton says, wanted to keep the fur trade for themselves, and they resented the need to share sparse supplies with the newcomers.

Whatever the reason, that autumn the Weston men left and founded a village of their own, at the place called Wessagussett. The name means 'at the edge of the rocks', and so it is: a few hundred yards from the settlement site, close to the shore lie a cluster of rocks exposed at low water. Today Wessagussett goes by the name of North Weymouth, beside an Atlantic inlet called the Fore River, ten miles south of downtown Boston. Like many another colonial location, the banks of the Fore River have long since become industrial, lined with oil tanks, a power plant, and what was once a naval shipyard. Nonetheless, the geography survives, never entirely subdued, and the seascape retains its beauty, with the familiar New England counterpoint of overcast eggshell skies and speckled sandy woods.

As so often, at first the site seems unremarkable, just a small wooded dell beneath a low ridge. Between the ridge and the high-water mark was a flat strip of land about two hundred yards wide, and on it they established the Weston colony. Today white suburban houses cover the slopes and obscure the view inland, while a low concrete seawall defends the houses from the tide. But the ridge screens out the noise from the highway, and so with the help of old maps and a little imagination it is possible to appreciate the qualities of the place.

It was defensible, because North Weymouth is a peninsula between the curves of the Fore and Back rivers. Marshes and swamps left only a narrow neck of dry land along which it could be approached on foot. Wessagussett had excellent access by sea, because the Fore River made a good natural harbour. Sheltered from storms by islands and by a promontory to the east, the river has a grey sandy bottom, ideal for anchors. At low tide a wide expanse of mud and sand offered shellfish for the taking, and Wessagussett was renowned for oysters and mussels. The islands were rich with berries, and lobsters filled the bays and coves. Besides the availability of food, the site had a fourth attraction, freshwater. The dried-up bed of a stream can be found straying down through the dell to the sea.

In many ways Wessagussett outshone New Plymouth as a place to live. It was also far closer to the principal rivers of southern New England, the Charles, Mystic and Merrimack which led inland towards opportunities for trade. But unlike New Plymouth, Wessagussett was not an empty space. Its qualities rendered it ideal as a village site for the people of the Massachusetts, and some of them already lived nearby. Most visible among them were Wituwamat and Pecksuot: two tough and courageous men, determined to protect their domain, but occasionally brutal too. They made short, cruel work of the ship's company of two French vessels that had ventured into the adjoining waters.

When the first ship ran aground, the warriors made servants of her crew. They forced the Frenchmen to eat food fit only for dogs, until they wept and died. When the second ship arrived, hoping to trade, the warriors pretended to bring a bundle of beaver skins, and then with hidden knives they murdered her crew as well. The master of the ship put up a fight, hiding in the hold, and so they burned him out, butchered him too, and incinerated his vessel.

Settling in this dangerous location, Weston's men swiftly built houses and a palisade, but they had arrived too late in the year to plant corn. So, that November, the Pilgrims and the new arrivals used the *Swan* to make a joint expedition in search of corn and beans, intending to buy them from the native people in exchange for knives, scissors and beads. They intended to sail around the elbow of Cape Cod, south through the shoals, and then westward towards Buzzards Bay, but the weather was bad, and the shoals as baffling and treacherous as before. Then, as they traded near the modern town of Chatham, the Pilgrims lost Tisquantum.

In the words of William Bradford, he 'fell sick of an Indyean feaver, bleeding much at ye nose (which ye Indeans take for a simptome of death) and within a few days dyed there'. It has been argued that Tisquantum was poisoned, but this is no more than conjecture. His was only one of many deaths in 1622, in what seems to have been another epidemic. According to another source, the native people suffered another 'great plague', Standish went down with a fever but survived, and Weston's brother-in-law, one of the new settlers, died suddenly at New Plymouth. Massasoit himself fell gravely ill soon afterward, with a similar nosebleeding symptom.

Whether or not Tisquantum died of natural causes, his death removed the man who knew the English best, thanks to his period in London, a city where he had probably spent more time than any of the surviving Pilgrims, bar Winslow and Brewster. Indeed, if we wish to speculate, it is not impossible that as a business venture the voyage of the *Mayflower* was partly Tisquantum's idea. At the house of John Slany and at Merchant Taylors' Hall, Tisquantum would have been very conspicuous. It is inconceivable that he would have escaped the attention of the investors who backed the voyage.

It also appears from the Newfoundland Company's papers that Slany was a sympathetic host who would have listened carefully to what Tisquantum had to say. But this is a guess, and no more. We do know that in losing Tisquantum, the Pilgrims lost their finest translator and their best intermediary. When he passed away, they abandoned the trading expedition to the south.

Instead, less ambitiously, the *Swan* sailed back to the north, to trade in Boston Harbor, and then along the inside of Cape Cod Bay between the modern towns of Barnstable and Eastham. So they spent the autumn and the winter. Standish and Bradford made more forays in search of corn, by boat or overland. And as they did so, it became increasingly clear that they and Weston's men had antagonised the native people of the region. The most alarming incident occurred in March 1623. It involved Miles Standish.

Recovered from his sickness, in a small boat Captain Standish rounded the headland that forms the southern end of Plymouth Bay, on his way to the native settlement of Manomet. His task was to collect corn that Bradford had purchased. Standish found the corn, but not the cordial welcome he expected. He walked up from the beach to the house of the local sachem, taking with him two or three of his men but prudently leaving the rest with his boat. He had been at the house only a little while when in came two warriors from Wessagussett.

One of them was Wituwamat, the killer of Frenchmen. He took the English dagger he carried around his neck, a dagger confiscated from Weston's men, and he gave it to the sachem. Then he spoke at length, in riddling language that Standish could not comprehend but that the sachem greeted with enthusiasm. As Winslow tells the story, Miles Standish knew that an insult was intended, and most likely something far worse. Among the guests that night was a warrior from the Pamet River, a man who in the past had treated him as a friend. On this occasion, he boasted that he had a great kettle 'of some six or seven gallons'. He said that he would happily give it to the Englishman, as though the colonists were poor inferiors.

Refusing their invitation for his men to come up to the house, Standish hurried back to his boat, paying women from the village to carry the corn down to the water. The man from the Pamet insisted on coming with him, to sleep with the English. Fearing an assassin's knife, Standish remained awake, pacing up and down throughout a freezing night, in the orbit of his campfire. The following morning Standish sailed straight back to New Plymouth with the corn. It seemed that a crisis was approaching. In the eyes of William Bradford, the blame lay fairly and squarely with Weston's men at Wessagussett.

That winter, they began stealing food from the native people who lived nearby, digging up their storage pits at night. How many thefts there were is a matter for controversy. Bradford and Winslow suggest that there were several. Thomas Morton mentions only one, when a settler found a native barn in the woods and took a capful of corn. But even a single case of theft would be enough to gravely damage the reputation of the Pilgrims. Far from showing them to be rich and powerful, endowed with special skills, it would suggest that the English were small, shabby men, forced to barter or to steal. Worst of all, stealing was the opposite of giving; and for the native people of the coast, the surest sign of honour was generosity.

A decade or so later, somewhere in this region, the English radical Puritan Roger Williams witnessed a *nickommo*, a ritual feast or dance. At its heart lay the making of gifts, and it was the act of giving and not of receiving that brought good fortune. As Williams wrote, the hosts of the *nickommo* would 'give a great quantity of money, and all sorts of their goods, according to and sometimes beyond their estate ... and the person that receives this gift, upon the receiving it, goes out, and hollows thrice for the health and prosperity of the party that gave it, the master or mistress of the feast'. We can begin to see what the warrior from the Pamet was saying when he boasted about the great kettle that he said he would give to the English soldier. He was taunting Standish about the poverty of the colonists, and about their lack of means to make ritual donations.

He mentioned a kettle because kettles made of brass or pure copper had long been some of the most sought-after European goods. A document in the British National Archives serves to make the point. The ship's master who warned the Pilgrims about the native uprising in Virginia was John Huddleston, a man employed in taking emigrants to Jamestown and bringing back tobacco to the Thames. Sailing to America in 1619, he carried a hefty consignment of copper, weighing 'four hundredweight and four score pounds', in the form of bars and 'rundletts', meaning large kettles, mainly used at home for distilling brandy.

In native America, copper was more than just another mineral, and a kettle was more than a kettle. Some five thousand years ago, native peoples began smelting copper and using it to make knives, fishhooks and ornaments, in locations close to Lake Superior, where copper ore lay not far beneath the soil. Copper resists corrosion, it can be worked easily, and it shines with a luster that does not fade. Most precious of all was its colour, recalling the red of blood, making it a symbol of life, healing and fertility. Copper kettles were versatile, with many uses, for cooking, as urns for the bones or ashes of the dead, or as a raw material.

New England and the St. Lawrence lay far away from the copper of the Great Lakes, and so here copper had an extra scarcity value. Once again, the French were far ahead of the English in recognising its potential. From the archives of provincial France, the Quebec historian Laurier Turgeon found that as early as the 1580s, French and Basque ships' masters were bringing across the Atlantic copper kettles in their hundreds. Trading goods needed to be rich and plentiful, and so too did the gifts the Europeans were expected to make. But, as Bradford and Winslow frankly admitted, their stock was scanty, and poor in quality, compared with the ample French supplies of kettles, hatchets and clothing. As we shall see, it was only when the Atlantic ports of France were closed by war that the English were free to take the lead in North America.

For the time being, in the spring of 1623, the survival of the Plymouth Colony remained anything but guaranteed. The previous autumn, into the bay had come a ship called the *Discovery*. Her master sold the Pilgrims what stock he had, but many years later Bradford still ruefully recalled the high prices he charged for knives and beads, and the very low price he gave them for beaver pelts. Weston's men made the situation still worse by squandering their own supplies of food and trading goods.

In perhaps his finest piece of narrative, William Bradford remorselessly depicted the squalid failure of the colony at Wessagussett. In the end Weston's men sold their clothes for food, they sold their bedding, and at their worst, they abandoned their huts and scattered like nomads among the woods and along the shore, to live on clams and groundnuts. Weakened by hunger, one man was unable to free himself from the mud of the beach where he was foraging for shellfish. He was found dead, from exposure or drowned by the tide. Their leader took native women as concubines, or so it was said. Losing all fear of the English, and all respect, Wituwamat's people took what little food the colonists had found and stripped them of what blankets they had left.

Bradford wrote in what he calls a 'plain style', but this did not mean that he lacked artistry. A technical, literary term, 'plain style' referred to a mode of writing based on Latin models, and especially Seneca, a favourite author in the Plymouth Colony. Developed by authors such as Sir Francis Bacon, the plain style influenced the composition of essays such as those of John Robinson. It was a type of prose intended to convey some moral or religious lesson as forcefully as possible, using the familiar, material language of everyday life. So, in the long passage that describes the collapse of Wessagussett, Bradford writes with unusual power and intensity, filling three manuscript pages with long, loose sentences, the longest stretching to nearly two hundred words.

Written in Jacobean plain style, the sentences tumble and unwind through a maze of semicolons and subordinate clauses, their wandering syntax imitating the dissolution of the company of men at Wessagussett. Bradford gives these straggling paragraphs shape and coherence by framing his account with phrases from Scripture. As always, we have to read him with the Bible at our side. Without it, we risk missing entirely the point Bradford wishes to make.

'It may be thought strange that these people should fall to these extremities,' he writes in his opening sentence, and the word 'fall' takes us straight to the book of Genesis. We remain in that territory when Bradford describes with contempt the behaviour he found most humiliating: the readiness of Weston's men to enslave themselves. 'Others (so base were they) became servants to ye Indeans, and would cutt them woode, & fetch them water,' he writes, adapting verses from the book of Joshua that describe the bondage of the Canaanites. Nearly one thousand words later, Bradford rounds off the narrative with a proverb, the moral of the story, and one that again uses the same motif: 'A man's way is not in his own power, God can make ye weake to stand; let him that standeth take heed lest he fall.'

These sentences condense two verses from the letters of Saint Paul to the Romans and the Corinthians, while concealed inside them lies another hidden allusion to the wilderness between Egypt and the promised land. Bradford quotes almost verbatim from the tenth chapter of 1 Corinthians, where Paul referred to the sinful Israelites who ignored the law of Moses and turned to idolatry and fornication, suffering death as a result. When Bradford likened the journey of the Pilgrims to the crossing of the Red Sea, his message conveyed praise and celebration, overlaid with awe. The affair at Wessagussett was its wicked opposite.

An unholy, inverted image of the Pilgrim passage to America, the fate of the Weston colony served only to prove that its victims were outcasts, sinners damned to exclusion from the ranks of the elect. Since Bradford was a Calvinist, he believed that their fate was predestined, an episode of retribution that made manifest God's unswerving justice.

Does all this make William Bradford unreliable as a historian? Not really, since Bradford never pretended to be anything but a follower of Calvin, and we have other accounts of the same events, by Edward Winslow and by one of the Wessagussett men, Phineas Pratt. If anything, these narratives and Morton's make the Wessagussett story still more distressing. Morton dwelled at length on a notorious incident when Weston's men hanged one of their own number for stealing corn from the native people, in the hope of placating them. Bradford only mentions this in passing, but this was characteristic. For Morton, and even more so for Winslow, detail mattered for its own sake, or for the sake of the reader: for William Bradford, details took their significance from the spiritual lesson they taught.

The Healing of Massasoit

In the spring and summer of 1623, the Pilgrims drew back from the edge of catastrophe by restoring their prestige in the eyes of the native people. The means they used were a combination of humanity, violence, and faith. While the humanity was Edward Winslow's, the violence belonged to Miles Standish. The gesture of faith was a gamble, but it succeeded.

While Standish was at Manomet, the Pilgrims heard perhaps the worst news they could imagine. Word arrived that Massasoit was ill and close to death. Winslow recognised this as a moment of definition, when the colonists had to take the initiative, either to help their friend or to salvage something from the disaster that his death would mean. He swiftly travelled on foot the forty miles to Massasoit's village. There he found that sickness had struck not only the sachem, but also his people.

Edward Winslow was not a physician, and this was just as well. An English doctor would have opened Massasoit's veins and bled him, a painful, upsetting and useless process that could only have hastened his end. Instead, Winslow tried to feed Massasoit. For two days the sachem had neither eaten nor slept, and he had temporarily lost his sight. A practical man, Winslow happened to have with him what he calls 'a confection of many comfortable conserves'. These, one guesses, were pickled fish, pilchards possibly, used by the English as seamen's rations. With the point of his knife, Edward Winslow pried open the clenched teeth of Massasoit and shoved the pickles into his mouth.

Winslow would have liked to give him liquor too, brandy most likely, the universal remedy of Jacobeans. Sadly, he had dropped the bottle on the way. Instead, he dissolved some pickles in water and gave the sachem that instead. It worked. Within thirty minutes, the stricken sachem revived, and his sight returned. Massasoit gave orders for his men to fetch more supplies, chickens and another liquor bottle from New Plymouth. In the meantime, Winslow improvised again. Massasoit wanted game stew, but Winslow felt that his patient was not yet ready for it.

A man of brilliant intuition, Winslow concocted an odd bouillon of cornflour, strawberry leaves and sassafras and fed a pint of it to the grateful sachem. Soon Massasoit was happily sitting on his latrine, where he deposited three small turds. Winslow counted them carefully, telling his English readers about them in the book he published the following year. Relieved from his burden, the sachem went to sleep.

The following day, Winslow tended the others in the village who were sick, and then in the evening he shot a duck. He plucked it and sliced off its breast to make a broth to give to Massasoit. Unhappily, the duck in question was fatty, as ducks so often are. Winslow knew that duck fat could be nauseating, but Massasoit ate the broth just the same and threw it back up immediately. Then the sachem had another nosebleed, for four hours. Once again Winslow waited, knowing that the death of Massasoit might mean his end as well. Happily, the bleeding ceased, and the sachem slept again. When he awoke, Winslow washed and bathed him. Soon Massasoit was sitting upright and beginning to regain his strength.

Winslow's courage was all the more significant because so many people witnessed it. Reports that Massasoit was gravely ill had travelled a hundred miles and brought a host of visitors to watch his last moments. Instead, they saw him recover, and they heard his fulsome thanks. Reaffirming his alliance with New Plymouth, at a critical moment, the incident restored the reputation of the Pilgrims as men with some form of spiritual power, access to resources of some special, valuable kind.

Winslow says that the native people used the word *maskiet* to refer to the medicine he had given to Massasoit. Besides meaning medicine, the word *m'ask-ehtu* also meant grass, or a green thing, or something raw or uncooked. It connected the ideas of health, life, youth, and benevolent fertility. Winslow had something finer than a copper kettle: he had the power to channel the forces of nature into healing, and he had done so freely and generously, as one should.

On his way back to New Plymouth, he paused at the home of the sachem Corbitant, once an enemy of the Pilgrims who now welcomed him warmly. There for the first time Winslow talked about religious belief with the people of the region, a conversation he reported straight back to London. With not a trace of bigotry and no sign of a sneer, Winslow records that he discussed with them the Ten Commandments. They approved of all except the seventh, the prohibition of adultery, which they considered unrealistic. They agreed that the English God was the same as their own supreme power, the benign divinity they called Kiehtan, the Creator God from the warm southwest, bringer of corn, beans, and new life.

And yet the power of the English might have a darker side, and so too might their God. If the English could cure, they could also destroy.

The Killing of Wituwamat

Winslow's mission had been accomplished, but he returned to New Plymouth with another alarming message. Massasoit had revealed the secret of the insults endured by Miles Standish at Manomet. Angered by thefts of corn, and possibly too by the desecration of graves, the people of the coast had decided to push the English back into the sea. The alliance apparently included all the native people who lived along the coastline from Provincetown, around the arc of Cape Cod, and as far as the Mystic River. It seems that Wituwamat and Pecksuot had persuaded their own sachem to give the order for an attack on the colony at Wessagussett. It would be followed immediately afterwards by the annihilation of New Plymouth.

Confirmation of the story told by Massasoit soon arrived, carried by Phineas Pratt. As cold, hunger and sickness began to kill the men at Wessagussett one by one, their quarrels with the native people became ever more bitter. Pigs were killed, knives were drawn, and the native people taunted the English. From the woods, now white with snow, they watched and waited for the right time to strike. Overconfidently, Pecksuot made the error of threatening the English too blatantly, assuming that none of them would have the courage to try to flee to warn the community of Plymouth. On 23 March, 1623, Pratt did so, making his escape from Wessagussett, through the swamps between the Fore and the Back rivers, with his pack on his back.

As the crow flies, the distance from here to New Plymouth is about twenty-five miles, through the modern towns of Marshfield and Duxbury, but nobody could hope to cross it on foot in a straight line. The terrain consisted of alternating bands of woodland, relentlessly identical, with few landmarks. With the howling of wolves in his ears, Pratt had no compass, and clouds covered the sun. For navigation he had to rely on a brief sighting of the Great Bear. Cutting through the forest were three rivers. Their waters are shallow and slow moving, but salt marshes make the estuaries formidable obstacles to a man on foot, impassable at high tide. Not until three the following afternoon did Pratt reach his destination.

He arrived to find the Pilgrims already preparing an expedition for the relief of Wessagussett. The day before, as Pratt struggled through the swamps, the colonists at New Plymouth had convened their annual meeting. The leading item on the agenda was the threat of an attack. Should they try to forestall it with a preemptive strike? After long debate, they decided to leave the decision to

Bradford and Standish. They chose to take the offensive. Standish and eight men would sail to Wessagussett to rescue the settlers. They would kill Wituwamat, cut off his head, and bring it back to serve as a warning to any other enemies of the Plymouth Colony. It was a very small force, but Standish planned to use deception. He would pretend that he was on a trading mission.

Standish and his force found Weston's small ship, the *Swan,* empty and at anchor in the Fore River. They fired a musket. From the woods and the beach at Wessagussett there appeared some of the survivors of the colony, men who had left the palisade and were living in native wigwams. Unarmed and apathetic – 'like men senseless of their own misery', Winslow says – at first they denied that they needed help. Questioning them, Standish found that the best men among them were still at the plantation, and so he went to find them. He gave them rations of corn and offered them sanctuary at New Plymouth, but he also ordered them to remain inside their palisade and say nothing to the native people.

The weather was vile, with rainstorms. In the wet, an attack with muskets could not be made. And as they waited, one of Wituwamat's men came boldly up to Standish, carrying beaver skins to trade. He could soon tell that Standish had not come to do business, and he reported back as much to his comrades.

Once again, Wituwamat and Pecksuot made threats with their blades, boasting about their murders of Frenchmen and English alike. They came up to the palisade and sharpened their knives in the open. They waved them so close to the faces of Standish and his men that they could see every detail of the weapons. Edward Winslow records that the knife of Pecksuot was ground down at its tip like the point of a needle. That of Wituwamat had on the end of its handle the likeness of a woman's face. At home he had another, decorated with the visage of a man. With these knives he had killed the master of the French ship that had beached nearby.

The confrontation ended in bloodshed the following day. According to Thomas Morton, Miles Standish persuaded the two warriors to eat, serving them pork. Edward Winslow's version of events makes no mention of a meal, but somehow Standish managed to entice Wituwamat and Pecksuot into a room in one of the houses built by Weston's men. There was another warrior with them as well as Wituwamat's younger brother, aged eighteen. Standish had three of his men with him, and although much smaller than his opponents he also had surprise on his side. No sooner was the door fastened than Miles Standish ripped the stiletto from around Pecksuot's neck. As Standish grappled with him, finally stabbing him to death, the other three Plymouth colonists fell on Witu-wamat and the unnamed warrior. They killed them too, after a wild struggle for possession of the knives. Then the Englishmen took Wituwamat's brother and strung him up to die by hanging. They found and killed another native, and some of Weston's men killed two more.

About half a mile east along the shore from Wessagussett, a hill rises between the swamps and the river to a height of about 150 feet. Today it has a long view across the bay towards downtown Boston. There, most likely, they fought the last round of the battle. Seeing a column of warriors advancing to take the hill, Standish and his men raced them to the top. Standish got there first, and the warriors retreated, took cover, and let fly with their bows and arrows. Standish and his men squeezed off two musket rounds against a warrior who showed himself from behind a tree, aiming an arrow at the captain. The warrior fled back into the swamp. The fight was over, save for a last exchange of insults.

The battle of Wessagussett, if we can call it that, took the lives of seven men of the Massachusetts people. Two Englishmen fell, not in combat, but because they were Wessagussett men who had been living in a native village. They were killed by their hosts after news arrived of Wituwamat's death. All that remained was for Miles Standish to sever the warrior's head from his body and sail back with it to New Plymouth, where they mounted it on its spike and left it there throughout the summer to be seen by every visitor, including Massasoit. Delighted by the outcome, Bradford took one final step. He sent a blunt warning to Obtakiest, the sachem of the area around Wessagussett, telling him not to damage the houses or the palisade that Weston's men had erected. Any further plots against the English would be dealt with in the same determined fashion.

10

EPILOGUE

After the affair at Wessagussett, it would take five more years of strenuous effort for the Plymouth Colony to secure its future. More settlers arrived from the mother country, so that by 1627 the Pilgrim community numbered nearly 160, of whom more than a third were adult males. With this ample labour force, Bradford and his comrades could feed and defend themselves, and they had built a working relationship with Massasoit and his people. What they had not yet achieved was a trading profit. Only when they did so could their survival be guaranteed.

Their essential supplies – iron tools, ploughs and cattle, and arms, ammunition and gunpowder, not to mention copper kettles and other trading goods – all had to come by sea from England. Everything had to be paid for, sooner or later; but as each year went by, so the colony's debts increased. By the autumn of 1626, the old *Mayflower* investor consortium in London had given up hope of recovering the money they had sunk into the project. And so they struck one last deal with the Pilgrims.

In November of that year, the forty-one investors who remained agreed to write off all the equity capital they had invested in 1620. They also ripped up the onerous contract that Thomas Weston had devised, and they abandoned their claims on the Plymouth Colony's land, equipment and livestock. They added up the money the Pilgrims had borrowed, which came to £1,800 – very roughly equivalent to £1.5m, in 21st century money – and gave them until 1636 to repay it in annual instalments. In the meantime a few of the bravest men in the consortium, chiefly Beauchamp, Pocock and Sherley, would support the Pilgrims with new loans at high rates of interest.

It was an arrangement that might just do the trick, if William Bradford and the Pilgrims could at last begin to ship home the beaver skins that they had hoped to find. And this is precisely what happened. The colony's luck was about to turn.

In 1625, Edward Winslow had made a trading foray along the coast of New England to Maine and the valley of the Kennebec River. It was a promising location, where the native people had access to beavers in vast numbers. With their birch-bark canoes, the Abenaki people of the region were used to travelling hundreds of miles in search of game and furs. The rivers and streams that flowed into the Kennebec formed a huge system of waterways that reached deep inland, as far as the modern border with Canada, into forests and swamps ideal for the beaver. Because in the cold interior of Maine the growing season was short, the Abenaki often ran short of food, and so they were happy to sell their beaver skins to Winslow in return for surplus corn which the Pilgrims produced at New Plymouth.

From his first trip to the Kennebec, Winslow came home with the pelts of about 400 beavers. If he could do this again, year after year, the colony would have a fighting chance of meeting its liabilities. Not only did they have their corn to sell to the Abenaki. The Pilgrims had also discovered a new source of currency that could be used to buy beaver skins. It took the form of wampum, or white and purple beads fashioned from shellfish found along the coast of southern New England. It was greatly prized by the native people, who used the wampum to make long multi-coloured belts. Since the early 1620s, Dutch traders had been using wampum to buy furs in the Hudson valley, and they were willing to sell some of the wampum to the Plymouth colonists.

To make the best of these new opportunities, in 1627 and 1628 the Pilgrims established two new trading posts. One was located in southern Massachusetts at the western end of Cape Cod, where they could trade for wampum with the Dutch. The other was 200 miles to the north-east at Cushnoc, in the middle valley of the Kennebec, on the site of the modern city of Augusta, Maine. There Winslow could sell corn and wampum to the Abenaki trappers who came down the river with their beaver skins.

It was a bold manoeuvre by the Pilgrims but it succeeded brilliantly. The English Separatists who had sailed to America from Leiden had no religious objections to doing business. As an early Massachusetts historian put it in the 1680s, 'having lived with the Dutch in Holland, they were naturally addicted to commerce and traffic'. They also had the devil's own luck, because in 1627, as they began to pay off their debts to the consortium in London, the price of beaver fur in Europe was rocketing upwards.

For this the Pilgrims had to thank the kings of England and France. The old peacemaker king James I had died in 1625, to be succeeded by his son Charles I, who promptly went to war with Spain. And then in 1627 Louis XIII and his chief minister, Cardinal Richelieu, laid siege to the troublesome Huguenot stronghold of La Rochelle.

Soon England was at war with France as well, sending an expeditionary force to La Rochelle to try to raise the siege.

And so the Atlantic became a battleground, as English, French and Spanish warships and privateers did their best to plunder each others' merchandise. The price of beaver skins trebled in the space of three years. Each pelt shipped home from New England in 1628 fetched more than twenty shillings in London, and the price held firm until 1630. With their ample supplies of fur from Maine, at last the Plymouth Colony could turn a handsome profit.

It was just what the Pilgrims required. La Rochelle fell to the French crown, a crushing defeat for the Protestant cause which deeply alarmed William Bradford and his friends and their Puritan cousins at home in England, but the colony was safe financially. Not only could the Pilgrims pay their debts. They had also proved that their kind of colony, based on a combination of religious zeal, New World techniques of farming, and hard commercial graft, could survive on the North American coast. William Bradford and his comrades had built a viable prototype for much larger settlements that would follow.

In England in 1629, Charles I dissolved Parliament and embarked on eleven years of personal rule. Although it can be argued that the king was never quite the tyrannical villain that Puritan ideology would make him out to be, his religious policies alarmed his opponents who feared that he was bent upon making England a Roman Catholic country once again. But now they had a place of refuge to which they could sail. In London, Puritan merchants had closely followed the adventures of the Plymouth Colony. They could see how it worked and how it made its money. And so they drew up plans for a new, far more ambitious settlement in New England, to be financed in its early days by the beaver trade.

On 4 March, 1629, six days before the king sent Parliament packing, he granted a royal charter to a new American venture. It was the Massachusetts Bay Company. As the wars with France and Spain drew to a close and ships became available for business again, the Company began to assemble a fleet that could carry as many as 1,500 colonists. Under the command of the Puritan John Winthrop, it set sail for America in the spring of 1630. In September, Winthrop gave the name of 'Boston' to the largest of the settlements they founded in New England. The Great Migration of Puritans to America had begun. By the late 1650s there would be as many as 20,000 English settlers in Boston and its hinterland, elbowing aside the native people whose territory it was.

And what of William Bradford and the Pilgrims? As the years went by, Bradford served term after term as the Plymouth Colony's governor. The Pilgrims had achieved what they had set out to do, by creating a Protestant bridgehead in America; while at home in England, the Puritans had been still more successful, replacing the monarchy with Oliver Cromwell as the Lord Protector of the nation. And yet Governor Bradford was not an entirely happy man.

As the English colonies grew and prospered, so Bradford worried that in America they were succumbing to greed and forgetting the spiritual purpose that had led the Pilgrims on their errand into the wilderness. But that, as they say, is another story. In 1657, the year before Cromwell died, William Bradford passed away. They laid him to rest on Burial Hill, in sight of the sand dunes of Cape Cod across the bay.

VINTAGE CLASSICS

Vintage launched in the United Kingdom in 1990, and was originally the paperback home for the Random House Group's literary authors. Now, Vintage is comprised of some of London's oldest and most prestigious literary houses, including Chatto & Windus (1855), Hogarth (1917), Jonathan Cape (1921) and Secker & Warburg (1935), alongside the newer or relaunched hardback and paperback imprints: The Bodley Head, Harvill Secker, Yellow Jersey, Square Peg, Vintage Paperbacks and Vintage Classics.

From Angela Carter, Graham Greene and Aldous Huxley to Toni Morrison, Haruki Murakami and Virginia Woolf, Vintage Classics is renowned for publishing some of the greatest writers and thinkers from around the world and across the ages – all complemented by our beautiful, stylish approach to design. Vintage Classics' authors have won many of the world's most revered literary prizes, including the Nobel, the Man Booker, the Prix Goncourt and the Pulitzer, and through their writing they continue to capture imaginations, inspire new perspectives and incite curiosity.

In 2007 Vintage Classics introduced its distinctive red spine design, and in 2012 Vintage Children's Classics was launched to include the much-loved authors of our childhood. Random House joined forces with the Penguin Group in 2013 to become Penguin Random House, making it the largest trade publisher in the United Kingdom.

@vintagebooks

penguin.co.uk/vintage-classics